the mouthmark
book *of* poetry

literary pointillism on a funked-out canvas

the mouthmark book of poetry

Published by flipped eye publishing, 2013
www.flippedeye.net/mouthmark
All Rights Reserved

Cover Design
Series Design © flipped eye publishing, 2005

ISBN: 978-1-905233-15-1

the mouthmark
book *of* poetry

Nick Makoha • Inua Ellams • Jacob Sam-La Rose
Truth Thomas • Jessica Horn • Denise Saul
Malika Booker • Janett Plummer • Warsan Shire

introduction

The mouthmark project was a 5-year targeted poetry pamphlet series to unearth new poets from non-conventional traditions. Although, many of the poets published came from performance backgrounds, equally, majority had a cultural palette that extended beyond Western norms. Significant effort was invested in appreciating the unique influences that each poet carried before embarking on editorial work.

However, more than a scheme to give emerging poets a platform, the project was a quest for us to learn a new aesthetic, to be part of its creation – rather than accepting some predefined notion of poetry and fitting the submissions we received to it. We approached the task with the understanding that everything that is known about poetry derives from experiment, an act of artistic expression that yielded templates and theories. We made progress by being flexible, listening and learning along the way.

It is no coincidence that the mouthmark project has also been the training ground for our editors, with both Jacob Sam-La Rose and Niall O'Sullivan editing their first books for flipped eye under the project, and, recently, our intern from the University of Leicester, Cara Lai, doing the proofreading for this very anthology.

Importantly, the mouthmark project was a development period for the very poets we edited. We spent long months working on most of the pamphlets, sometimes years, and the routine was not exacting. We were led by a philosophy of letting poets learn their own aesthetics in the process; rationalise their own complex formations, derived from unique class and cultural juxtapositions, and how they affected their work; understand what elements of craft were important to them and how to leverage them effectively to augment their work. For example, the work of Truth Thomas and Jessica Horn pulls politics to the foreground, whereas Inua Ellams privileges musicality over politics; Warsan Shire's imagery draws one to a point of intensity, while Nick Makoha's images carry more of a centrifugal energy. These are, of course, only small elements in the amalgams that constitute each poem of theirs, but it demonstrates the danger of not letting poets find their way.

Because we were all learning, I do not believe any of the pamphlets in the mouthmark pamphlet series is perfect, but I can state with certainty that they are all moving, important markers in the careers of poets that have already begun to capture the world's attention, selling thousands of books and winning awards along the way. Our design concept, brown paper and black ink, was in fact our way of signalling that this was work that was right off the grill, rough and ready. Yet, what the readership and awards tell us, without doubt, is that the aesthetic we sought at beginning the mouthmark project resonates with the contemporary world. There is nothing that makes an editor prouder than to be part of something that moves the globe.

Nii Ayikwei Parkes
Senior Editor, flipped eye publishing

praise for the mouthmark pamphlet series

*"The mouthmark series — launched by independent publisher flipped eye
publishing in 2006 — has published the first pamphlets of many key Black
and Asian poets since it started. The imprint focussed on allowing artists
of diverse heritages to bring all their influences to the page, from hip-hop to
sports. In doing so it has challenged previous conceptions of what UK poetry
should/could do and demonstrated that poets have moved beyond distinctions
of page and stage, high and low culture to produce exciting new forms. The
poets were guided to produce high quality work designed to progress their
careers to full collections — a level of support not often offered by publishing
houses. The fact that so many of mouthmark's pamphlets have gone on to be
PBS winners or recommendations and that many of the artists have gone
on to major collections/international reputations, demonstrates the success
of this approach. It is also notable how many of the poets have been selected
by the Complete Works rounds I and II, a national development programme
supporting diversity and quality in British poetry. There is little doubt that
the imprint has had an impact on UK publishing, bringing many new poets
with distinct voices to the attention of the wider public."*

Nathalie Teitler
Director, The Complete Works project

*"During our annual search for suitable Aldeburgh Poetry Festival poets,
having discovered a poet's work we are always delighted to find that they have
been published by flipped Eye in the mouthmark series. It means we can be
confident that the poet has been rigorously edited and will have a book that's
beautifully designed and produced with care and attention. And that's a rare
and valuable thing."*

Naomi Jaffa
Director, The Poetry Trust

List of Titles

about Nick Makoha

Born in Uganda, Nick Makoha fled with his mother during the Idi Amin dictatorship. He has lived in Kenya, Saudi Arabia and currently resides in London. Nick represented Uganda at Poetry Parnassus for the 2012 Cultural Olympiad and his poem "Vista" was used in a video installation to promote the 2008 Turner Prize. His one man show, *My Father and Other Superheroes* had its debut at the 2013 London Literature Festival. A former writer in Residence for Newham Libraries, Nick was one of ten writers on an Arts Council-backed development programme called The Complete Works and was mentored by T. S. Eliot Prize-winning poet George Szirtes, as they are both writers in exile.

author statement

flipped eye where very daring in taking me on as the first poet in their mouthmark pamphlet series. I had no track record; my learning curve was steep but never once did they make me feel inferior. They don't just show a belief in the work they show a belief in the poetics and the artist. In the editing process, a daunting one for any writer, flipped eye mix honesty with optimism to build a rapport. Nii read all my work, however obscure, to get a sense of context. Wherever possible he did this in person at readings, cafes or bookstores. In flipped eye's stable, your work is supported to the ends of the earth and not just in the first year of publishing - they make the book a platform from which you, the writer, can stand. The Lost Collection of an Invisible Man really made a mark for me; it helped me see the writer I could become. For that I am humbled and thankful.

kudos

shortlisted for
the Arvon International Prize (2010)
the Troubadour Prize (2010)
selected as
Poetry Parnassus Poet, Uganda (2012)

The Lost Collection of an Invisible Man

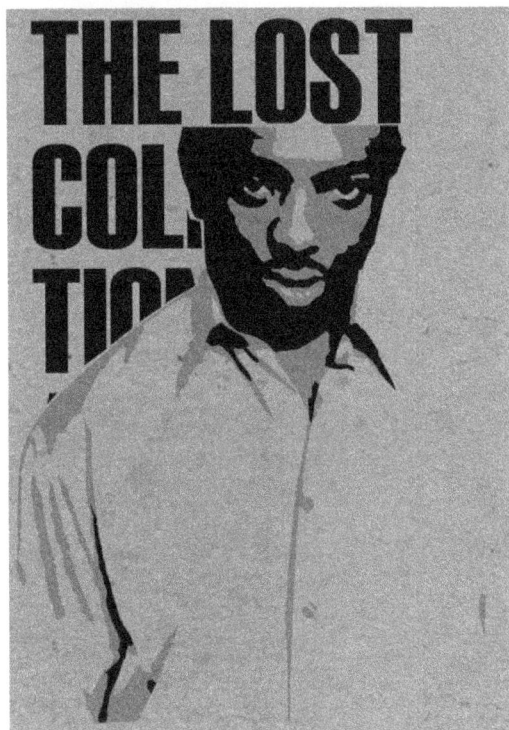

Nick Makoha

First Published: 2005
Series Number: 01
Editor: Nii Ayikwei Parkes

The Lost Collection of an Invisible Man

Najua

Sitting alone in December
a clock shaped from Uganda ticks.

My sixth birthday came
with smiles and memories.

Few furnish the house now;
I feel like a burden instead of a son;

love lost in translation
because I can't speak my mother tongue,

or Kiswahili. I have forgotten how to say I need you.
Miss the laughter, jokes and conversation.

Smiles and memories draped in suntan
return from Uganda, put on walls dressed

in weaved hairstyles. And maize meal
will spill itself into kitchen cupboards

from moving half-filled plastic containers
with lids not closed, to burning iron pots on hot gas fires

left in china plates, half eaten in cold fridges
from a market she went to with friends

who she would have spent all night with, packing,
                speaking in a language I no longer understand.

City Block

1

I used to love summer.
The sun would start in my room,
leave through my mother's skin.

If we had guests I got to sleep with her.
I remember the nights were cool,
I would wear t-shirts in them.

Tower blocks were the castles I lived in,
when Dunlop green-flash was cool.
Hip black was still the necessary enemy.

Back then the D.S.S. office was a cinema
and Kwik-Fit was a wholesale store.
Same neighbourhood different walk.

I used to wait for mum
to go to her cleaning jobs,
so I could play her old b-sides.

She didn't find out I broke
the needle till her birthday party.
She was too drunk to be annoyed.

I wore my pinstripe suit.
An eight-year-old Kojak look-alike,
without the lollipop.

Got to stay up past the nine o'clock news,
got to watch Starsky and Hutch before
pretending to fall asleep on the sofa.

I peed and blamed it on my cousin.
Living on the fifth floor was special,
the world to me was concave.

2

The snapping click of suitcases
never taught me to unpack.
I want some kind of guarantee

that if I close my eyes you won't disappear
and you won't turn into another stranger,
who can't pronounce my name.

Always wait for me at the end of a long day,
always kiss me into existence,
always stay right here where I need you.

Call me just to know what time it is,
argue so we can have something to fight about,
forgive me for forgetting my mother tongue.

I love you still sounds the same with this accent.
Even though you say you love the maps in my eyes,
you can't follow the roads that race across my skin.

You see, once I start I don't know how to stop.
I spin out the door into a whole new costume,
                        making it hard to love but easy to leave.

As for my thoughts, they are dreams dying.
Haven't been the man I said I would be for days.

Yet she still waits on edge of phone,
hair tucked behind ear for the movement.

Muscles tighten at the speed of thought,
as she fills the vacuum with concern

hidden in the question of: *How was your day?*
I bathe the fear of her leaving in laughter.

I know laughter better than I know her,
yet, I pretend what I said was fiction.

She pretends that my fiction were true.
Truly we are a story narrated by a liar.

I am the one who will not admit love;
like oceans organically raised by tears,

deceiving themselves that they were
born on the thighs of mountains.

Giving her a middle name because it feels good.
Spelling it backwards to hear what it sounds like.

Mimicking childhood till it becomes real laughter.
Who could forget laughter, the cousin of giggles?

The Light

The city clings like skin to the back of me.
Summer sweat, my oils mixing

with the humidity of the night.
Sleep the language I am speaking,

every move mimicking death.
My body leaves a signature

in the sheets. I rise; my feet touch the carpet's canvas
cooling me slightly. The window spilling moonlight

into the room. Artificial light born from the TV mimics
the light of the sky. Voices like my vision, blurred.

My hand snakes to the remote to mute the sound
that brought me to sleep and in this moment awakens me.

It is 3:58. My rubber tongue sticks to my mouth.
My movements wake her; she sits up from the pyramid of pillows

that support her back. Reaching for her brow, I comfort her
holding her ripe belly, filled with our child.

As quiet as the night is, my dreams are still fresh in my mind.
I hear voices through the refracted mirror of the TV.

A child is being born. I have been dreaming
about my child; it was a girl this time.

My hand still rests on her belly as flickering shadows
walk across the wall. I hear peace for the first time.

I look at her knowing that in five weeks I will
be that father on the TV.

The catalyst of the night, muted TV, sweat and
my girl in my bed bring these thoughts to me often.

Her sigh calls me to bed. Sweat painted on sheets evaporates.
I lean into cooled sheets; she switches off the TV.

Leaving us with the light of the moon.

Motto

Picking up the phone I hear it.
She is known for her tears;

days don't go by without them.
It's her way of telling you she loves you.

She hides it well, like
the pain of her first abortion

it's bookmarked under failure.

Words loosen from her stomach

travel up through her chest
reminding her of truth she lives by.

Her first and second loves left her
decisions – to raise or kill a newborn.

Forgiveness rests uneasy on her shoulders
God only belongs to those who believe.

Some syllables travel to her throat
but the anger hums vowels to tears.

Words cannot reclaim the silence
Goodbyes only punctuate the   space .

What's On God's Mind

How many sleepless nights must I tolerate
to avoid dreams being taken away?

In Turi, Africa I used to
walk across radio waves,

to hear how maize has left the soil
like a battered wife leaves her husband.

My laughter is a swollen lie;
I use the the sound to chase

the memory of my dad from my mind.
It's a dream hidden in the loss of words.

Losing my faith in facts;
hiding tears in abstracts

Resenting the days in boarding school
I had to unpack feelings in a stolen jar

Sitting on school steps
wishing other mothers would steal my heart.

Making jokes to hide the scars.
Humour never erased the pain.

I see my father's streak in my life
It's why I never look a woman straight in the eye.

Dad lives a flight away
or a phone call my mother will never make.

Their only proof that love exists is me.

Sinai

If I lose you at the water,
I will find you at the mountain.
You know how I thirst,
But I've got to get high first.

There is a river where waters are daylight
A soul whose springs are nightshade
And a land where the two waters meet
Joy as my love bathes in these pools.

She introduced herself as all my next breaths
Her dreams auditioned to become my realities
Forcing me to exhale all my sufferings.
I tried to exist in the perfumes of my yesterdays
But found she had stitched her name in the collar of my soul.

Yet every time I showed her my love
She hid in her wounds
And camouflaged the tears
That watered the garden of her days.

Her deepest memories started to assume
That I too was groomed
in the armour of her past loves
Who had scarred her heart with a sword of promises

I was crucified for such care
Still, in the silence that binds all these moments together
I tried to, believe me, I tried to
keep this echo inside myself

That is when the mountain moved.

My Cousin

Kenya was not as green as I remember.
Landing on tarmac that melts to toffee,
my western attire made me a target.
Customs thought me dressed in money.
They wanted money and opened my bag,
they wanted money, silence.

I remember my mother screaming on the phone.
I thought she was laughing with her friends.
I grew up with him like a brother, like a son,
lived in his mother's house, did dance routines.
Was there when his father died, became the man.
Two days later we were on a plane.

We'd eat in the room with the gold clock.
At one sitting, eating three meals straight.
Thick Ugali cake and sukamawicke
that should have lasted a week; we ate it in a day.
Eating loaves of bread just to race,
with Kenyan tea made with milk, not water.

In a stone church with wooden murals,
his body was carried to the side of the altar
as a burden on the shoulders of his cousins.
Friends and acquaintances filled the church,
spilling outside from all doors and exits.
Dignitaries and locals stood side-by-side.

I went straight to the coffin that lay in the dining room,
stared at him for ages. Old men held children.
He looked so peaceful. Mothers held loved ones.
Like on school mornings when he couldn't wake.
Everyone carried on like it was just another day.
Lonely tears came later on my return, at Heathrow.

Psalm

I have been to heaven and back twice
Seen God comb the stars to peer through your eyes
Wrestled with the Devil to possess your caress
To perform your love as mine

I have tamed the sun from its burn
Taught wisdom to recognise who you are
Infected dreams with your memory
And drawn your heart in the storm

I have anointed my spirit with your name
Nurtured my joy to soak your pain
Neglected my joy for your foolishness
Washed my transgressions in the pool of your divine mind
To perform your love as mine

I have spoken my love in tongues
Hidden secrets in prophets' arms
Instructed your oppression to claim my freedom as thine
To perform your love as mine

The Necessary Enemy

Having come to glory's end,
inheritance spent on rule-breaking,

in the car's back-seat sits
a coward clothed in ulcers,

hoping your words will cure
the pinch of acid in my tears

The Lost Collection of an Invisible Man

Once a cloth, now a rag
I have folded 30 years.

People clean their bodies
with my life as their love.

Understanding distance,
I appreciate slow motion.

Losing hair, like loss of love,
out of my control, both I fear.

The only taboo in a desert is rain.
My rain, kindness within a desert of friends.

My heart learns to balance
these words in your ear.

The Currency of Truth

Listen to the voice not the words,
the currency of truth,
it's the only thing you can take with you.

Smiles are in your architecture.
I'm scared of the fear of becoming important.
You might find out I am a fake.

Like when I changed my name as years change the days,
to give myself a sense of history.
Maybe I could be joined to you by love, our child, my actions, by words?

You told me you could not be found in my poems,
so I carve myself out of this page.
I don't believe in god but you show me holes in your hands.

I will build you a window on the 13th floor,
paint myself on the inner wall of your right lung,
I would saw myself in two, to hold these words to your ear.

This love could be a painted dream;
I could be there for you,
but find it hard to be there for myself.

Doing it yourself fits badly together,
but I'll learn to use my hands
to build a world for us that is more than wallpaper.

The first time we held hands you slept in this bed,
I slept beside you, eyes closed, body awake.
Took a year for us to make love, too busy being friends.

Other guys watch you when you talk;
what's funny is you think I am beautiful.
You look good even when you're angry,

late at night 2 o'clock in the morning,
when your venom is the only sound in my ear,
the silhouette of your back resting on my shoulders.

It's the first time I realised you could die.
But what if I die, will you be okay?
All that's important in this whole world:

I love you; have the pictures to prove it.
Pictures are my house of love –
I want our child to have these kinds of pictures.

An eight-by-ten picture sits on my TV
taken in photo booth, your eyes swollen from crying,
smile warm from loving, head resting on mine.

Building the memories now they'll keep coming.
There's nothing I can do to keep you,
only honesty will make you stay.

Our child links us for eternity;
even if I die today I'd still exist to you.
If you die the only proof I'll have of your existence is our child.

The sadness of that bothers me.
These are things you'd like to hear,
but I never say because I don't want to feel that sadness.

True reason, bad excuse.
Listen to the voice not the words;
it is the only thing you can take with you.

Yellow Sands

She looks more beautiful
when she lets her locks fall.

On asking, she says unconvincingly
that the mornings are way

too short to comb her hair.
But I have seen her spend

the amount of time in the bathroom
it takes the 8.29 train

to get from Victoria to Thornton Heath.
She doesn't like to breakfast

unless I am there.
On my arrival her smile alters moods,

turning tiredness into conversation.
Why use oil when we can use words,

exchange fingers for tongues? Sighs can remain.
As much as I love her body, it's the way she says things

like *yellow sands make islands beautiful;*
three days of lovemaking can't replace

the way she says my name at the edge of a phone.
She changes me from a brick to a cornerstone.

Refraction

The world is a canvas I can't see behind.
Closed eyes cannot lift me from this earth.

My might not strong enough to ask for forgiveness,
hand bent back in agony rejects the curvature of the back.

Delivering crimes in the time it takes
an envelope to move around the world.

Like light, I should bend the moment;
through the lens of the past,

create an image of the time when
lovers' laughter was their only crime.

Beauty, hers to give and mine to receive,
and her twenty-fifth birthday,

when gifts came in sets of seven
and phone calls preceded text messages.

But the light will not bend that far;
only to the bed with this body, this skin.

Pain In My Back

At my your funeral
there were tears from my mother's eye.
She shared them with my aunt;
her sister, your mother, my friend.
Mine were late.

Felt like they didn't belong in Africa,
like rivers and streams don't belong to the land.
This is the story I tell to hide my pride.
Words glued to the inside of my mouth,
unable to tell your corpse I love you.

Your face now inflamed,
void of soul scares me;
like my seven-year-old nightmares.
If I closed my eyes you would
peer right into my soul.

Didn't want you or god to know
I envied the kindness
radiating past your buckteeth
and perfectly round face.
I am not you.

Tripped you for fun when you were skipping.
The head bump turned your face into Janet Jackson's.
Your father, also dead, beat the life out of me.
Still, no tears. I chose to be angry;
hid the pain in my back.

The remembrance of the pain now laughable,
when compared to the loss of you.
I say this to you in English

but my tears speak Swahili.
I wish your father could beat the life out of me,

so I could join you.

Who Do They Say That I Am?

They say that I am
Three words short of a proverb;
Two beliefs less than a religion;
One god less to believe in.

They say that I am
Three tribes short of a people;
One heart less of a couple;
Two breaths closer to death.

They say that I am
Three friends short of Judas;
Two betrayals less than Brutus;
One wisdom short of Confucius.

They say that I am
Three sins over temptation;
Two generations behind emancipation;
One prayer beyond frustration.

They say that I am
Three tears short of a river;
Two waters deep of leaders;
One hope less of a believer.

They say that I am
Three chains left of a slave;
Two victories short of the brave;
One coffin right of the grave.

about Inua Ellams

Born in Jos, Plateau State, Nigeria in 1984, Inua Ellams is a poet, playwright and performer. He has seven published books of poetry and plays including 'Thirteen Fairy Negro Tales'. His first play 'The 14th Tale' (a one-man show which he performed) was commissioned by the Battersea Arts Centre and awarded a Fringe First at the Edinburgh Festival, before a sold out run at The National Theatre in England. His third play, 'Black T-Shirt Collection' also sold out it's run at the National Theatre in 2012. His second pamphlet of poetry is called Candy Coated Unicorns and Converse All Stars and he is working on a new pamphlet and a first collection.

author statement

Thirteen Fairy Negro Tales was written as a dare. After the initial first title poem, a friend dared my to actually write thirteen poems in the same vein and its free formed, careening, loose, wild energy powered me through the writing process. When I'd finished, I had created something raw. I was 19 and knew very little about setting words down for the page, I was far more interested in musicality and at the time wrote mostly for the ear. I worked with Nii Parkes over months and the process was meticulous, considered, illuminating, at times, hard core, harsh, educational and entirely necessary. Without his innate understanding of who I was and what I was trying to do, the book would not exist.

kudos

winner of
Fringe First Award (Edinburgh, 2009)
longlisted for
the Alfred Fagan Award (2010)

Thirteen Fairy Negro Tales

Inua Ellams

First Published: 2005
Series Number: 02
Editor: Nii Ayikwei Parkes

Thirteen Fairy Negro Tales

Thirteen Fairy Negro Tales

I spun 13 fairy Negro tales that night.
Weighed them on illogic scales
that tipped the balance
and formed an alliance
with my version of the truth,
I uprooted reality and substituted it
for another that had more humanity;
thinking that if I thought hard enough
I'd make it real.

Having so much belief in mind power
I cowered beneath the defunct light
and attempted to bend Saturn's rings
around my mind.
I did this till the blinds let light in
to wake me from that super sonic slumber.
I swore I was under the influence of lightening
that struck my brain and convinced me I could stain worlds at a time.

But I realized it was just beer and wine.

I found I could dine on the sun
drink the milky-way
let stars stick to my tongue
clasp Orion around my waist
pluck Pluto, paste him to Mars and run
before Zeus realized I had face-lifted his estate.

I found I could reverse 360
from the 3 point line
and dunk Jupiter in a black hole.
But this divine world existed
only in my soul.

So I held my 13 Negro tales
and made a back bone
swapped it for my own
stood to the wind and dared earth
to spin me off it shoulders
not knowing I had soldered my pen to its core
and "ink"-planted a metaphor.

And perhaps this was just in my mind,
but I'd envisioned my self as a poet, so let it be
'cause I write this not for you,
just for me.
I'm trying to make the world a lil' better
by building bridges out of letters
trying to break the sound barrier
and obliterate the color lines,
'cause I was taught race was in the mind:
You can unwrap the illusions and unwind
to the sound of rainbow drops falling
on all proletarian props.

I speak thus
for I fell in love with an Iranian
girl who complimented my soul.
She had no color;
just a diamond backbone.
I looked in her eyes and saw five stories
for each tale I owned.
Though we never dated,
she sowed a seed in me
and I reap the fruits regularly
and mix the juice with ink,
so when I write about love
it tends to smell of her.

She is my virtue and my curse.

I guess I'm a fairy tale less now,
guess I have to chill at bus stops
and smoke sess now,

guess I have to trail blaze
and be like "yes now"
to every soul who gazes at me
trying to guess how
I can talk to myself and care less
about the effects of stress.
It's cause Spokenword is like sex,
the more you listen,
the better it gets.

That's why on long bus rides,
I close my eyes and try to hear drumbeats
from Nigeria- the motherland calling.
I be like "yes mum, I'm hearing ya."
It's like some ciphered world
with armies of sounds
and underground cultures
with talon-less vultures
trying to pierce my skin
and place talking drums within.

But Hip Hop takes over
and my head bobs to the beats
of a different soldier
and it's gotten colder
on this side of thought
'cause now,
I hear dreams money bought.

Driven despondent by this
I close my eyes tighter and
think a little deeper.
I see aquatic worlds
ruled by Soulquarians,
gods that remix bubbles with beats
so we inhale music
swap smiles for CDs
do voodoo just for the hell of it
and there is no pressure
if you choose to be celibate.

That's another fairy tale gone.
That's another scenario
I'd offered to the Sun
to run on Monday mornings
when workers are still torn
between workdays and fun.

A world without guns
when the only people running
are kids chasing nuns
for trying to convert them
when their teeth where still gums.
But the sun shrugged his shoulders
and shoved my idea where he couldn't see.
Telling me the cosmos didn't agree,
telling me humanity needed drama
in order to be free.
So I popped my middle finger
for Martin Luther King,
Seamus Heaney and Palestine's plea,
'cause you shouldn't need to suffer
to be granted mercy,
post-depression insurrection
is not a way to be.

But this world exists
between the purple evenings
that serve as backdrops to my reasoning
and nestle hopes of seasoning the world
with constructive dope,
to raise minds to that nexus in the sky
distill the plexus and finally understand
why Tupac, Biggie and Jim Morrison had to die.

I guess I'm more fairy tales less now
guess it's best if I tell you the rest now;
like how roots are looped through violin strings
and red mists faded yellow yell:
"the last bohemian lives!"...

like how Alice never loved in Never Land
and The last Rebels rise to remix riffs…

But the last fairy story
goes a bit like this:
I sit on a mountain top
with my Iranian scented ink
trace words on winds
sink to blue worlds
drink nectar
and think…

   and
      think.

Gangsters, Geishas and Goat Herdsmen

Once upon a time
in a kingdom of thought
on the death bed of parchment
along the pathways of discovery
uncovered in the blind movements
of a mind that dared to move men;

from the random scribbling
of a search for meaning and insight
a dying pen wrote revolutiona-realistically
of a secret carved into the rock face of life.

It reads of a concept,
conducive to the conquests of cohorts
conspiring to keep human hope alive.
It is divine intellect
base-lined in bridging the gaps
from gangsters and gats
to Mongolian goat herdsmen grazing
growing geishas star-gazing and
a girl with a gift in her grasp.

It reads, *We are all reflections of each other*.

I believe this to be true.

I believe that the might
of a medieval blacksmith
moulding metal in a forge
whose mystic assistance stretches
no further than a hammer's scourge
is reflected in the endless courage
of a working class mother making hot meals
in both of her dead end jobs.

I believe that the fear of a hood-rat
tasked with stealing five cars; that pressure
that doubt, that pause…
is found in a ballet dancer with already red toes
asked to pirouette through five bars.

I know that when a drunk hits rock bottom
when light sears through the undergrowth
of his reality and he sees truth
that moment of sudden clarity
is mirrored in the seconds a scientist spies
the last lines of a mathematical thesis
and turns it into truth.

I know that once
in the courtyards of colour
a glimmer from the fortress of thought came forth
bearing notions of using pure hues on canvas.
That was the birth of Impressionism.
A reflection of that movement
moved MCs to remix their mental motions
and that was the birth of Hip Hop's keeping it realism.

And Behold!
On the balconies of the Age of Aquarius
it shall be told
that of the many soldiers that have fallen
few rode bold into battle convinced
by the reasons for which they fought.
That fact is reflected in the life struggles
of every day people.

This uncertainty spawns the freethinkers,
the 'Freaks'
and the fury of the last bohemian
screaming "power to those freaks"
is a reflection of the fury
with which I write

I WRITE IN THUNDER SPEAK!

that turns lightning to mere weather
glows so my word plays
could be the earth glows that bathe
thought flows into submission.

My mission is to be the very best
that I can be. So often at street corners
I speak to locals, grab the essence
of their spirits in a choke hold and squeeze
till their truth emits from my vocals;
so I can walk the waking
woe calls of we
and find a new me
in the voices of others.

So if by the end of this
you don't believe in a reflection
of yourself, just trust
that your soul has been lathered
across the cusps of mirrors world wide
and within him, her or me,
you can find an image of yourself.
Because collectively
we reflect infinity amongst
ourselves, living
happily
ever
after.

Mono Moveism

Thousands of feet from the death
place of Icarus, miles from wilting
wet wax wings and water crystals freezing
to nothingness; of the tribe of Israel, lying
between the lands of Judah and Azekah
weather beaten into rank, flanked on both sides
by faceless rebel rubies

there is a pebble
that remembers Goliath
there is a sling that remembers victory
there is a song that remembers joy.

Under sharp stones and bare feet
under dusty courtyards and half buried secrets;
five steps from misplaced identities
and misled theories
two miles from dry prayer mats
and interstellar symbols called into life
by a Muslim man, mauling the wind
with soul-bred callings to prayer
peppered by bullet-shaped words
and wicked agendas on weary nights;
wrought of wood, buried six feet under
loose gravel and broken pillars of hate

there is an empty plate
that remembers Ghandi,
there is a linen cloth
that remembers death.

In the citadels of ancient Greece
past the stone monuments to myths and legends

that guard the gateways to gods and goddesses
past perforated pillars and perennial peeling
frescoes that flake;
behind that, behind the fountains that flicked water
on sweat-wetted marble;
in the corner ruins of a bath house
bathed in unbroken peace
unscathed and partially scripted

there is parchment
that remembers Plato,
there is a pen
that remembers thought.

And through that, look.
Look to the last century, from Georgia's red hills
to the mole hills of Mississippi, from the mountains
of New York, to the peaks of California, look.
From the snow capped Rockies of Colorado
to the deserts of Texas, look.
Through race riots, flaming crosses
and chain gangs clad in white, through night
through prayers whispered from bruised lips
through knees bent, lips locked
through sentences to death
and besetting breath, look.
Through empty seats at the backs of buses
and bent resurrections of hope, through courage
eloping with strength, through lengthy winters
and withered minds through conviction unwinding
to a backdrop of bedraggled Bibles
covered in blood,
    "though weeping may endure for a night,
    joy comes with the morning"
so look through it.
Look to the coming of the Sun
and spirits soaring through sound
look through a million men marching
with fists thrown up!

Married to that memory
there is a microphone
that remembers Martin Luther King
there are men that still dream.

And in the basements of moth eaten project buildings
beneath black bohemian bookshelves
and brown bathrooms, there is a backroom
baptized with sweat and tears.
Before it, an un-vacuumed space
filled with broken boom boxes,
archaic electronics and drumsticks
resting on dead drums gone humdrum
interwoven with expired wires and quiet
speaker boxes that peak through the shadows.
Caught amongst this current of silent
symphonies of rare riffs and rivers of rough
rhythms, rounded with dust

there is a fractured needle
that first free styled funk
there is broken vinyl that remembers flesh
there is a deck that remembers Grand Master Flash…

These men are testaments to the notion
that one man can make a movement
one child can start the change
so as this poem reaches its range
believe that beneath your clothes beats
a heart that beats to the backdrop of destiny
believe that you possess the power
you are the form of suns, believe that
your actions can cause a reaction that snowballs
into an avalanche of word wide will
and by your movements
someday, we may reach that zenith
of happily, ever, and after.

Midnight Music Marauders

If music be the food of love, play on.

And we played on that night.
Like a mellow cello player, high
on milk and melanin, making
bone marrow music, we played
like a sparrow musing on Beethoven
using the borrowed wings of wordless
words, absorbing Gaia through fingers
probing, blunt swords through soft butter.

We played like a guitar riff
uttered from Venus, shuddered
from the rocking shoulders of a colour
blind pianist, like a stream of beauty
seam-less, we played like the seamstress
of sound sewing soul-quaric pulses
in the lands of eardrums, drawing treble clefs
on brown cliffs, clawing at soaring notes
daring them to lift our spirits.

We played like a dead French kiss reincarnated
as a saxophone with tendencies to hiss
galaxophonic secrets through the tombs of trombones
reborn as the lower bones of Bojangles, dancing
on base drums prancing like songs of the railroad
set free, we played like freedom, stirring
on those hills reflected in the back heels
of a dancer in New Orleans
tapping prosperity

on concrete;
we played like the rose that grew
from concrete.

With its roots looped in violin strings
strung through harmonicas, planted in the wind
whistling tales of smelling just as sweet
weeping wet willows of wonder through pillows
producing sounds that slunk silently into darkness
we played like the Moonlight.
We were The Music.
We Danced.
Like two zephyrs with a license to live
later lolling like two lullabies, childlike
and moronic, stereophonic, hydrophonic
like a tonic squeezed from xylophones fed
to a young horn blower, blowing harmonious
tones of one to a cloud communion
resulting in a light rusty rain…

We played like rain-dust falling
dusting backstreets and high rise
buildings with homeopathic water
causing memories of Marvin Gaye, Jackson Five
Sam Cooke, The Supremes, Steve Wonder;
and we left that. We left the old memories
of Motown and came to the happenings of now
became two turntables spinning infinity
using incense sticks as needles
scratching divinity from vinyl, revealing
a soft state of existence we never knew existed.

    Like being caged in a marshmallow
    being tied with smoke
    being Saturn's sun-stroked
    being lathered by a rose

We became of the fellows with no sense
of reality- I became the bass drum
and she became that rhythm, adlibbing
free-flowing, free-styling, mad-living
like a symphony growing through hoops
entwining with its bass beginning roots.

That night, we played like a quartet
of dare devils drunk on Jasmine Juice
pulse- racing, temperature- rising
heartbeats audio-basing
in a big brilliant bang of blue
music, like a bison billowing through fog

And by the dying light, we parted with a hug
leaving the ghosts of galaxies
to congregate around our echoes
and create new worlds
from our laughter patterns
and live happily
ever
after.

Royal Displacement

Once upon a time
in a Kingdom far away
there lived a queen
with star maps in her palms.

She walked as one born in the third creek
from which the Nile eventually crept
she aired the essence of calm
capped in pupils as deep as psalms
from which she drew the secrets of life
and placed them in spoken shadows
for generations to reap and swallow
till wisdom wallowed
in the centres of their thought.

She had but to breathe out of beat
and sons darker than blue
would surround her in her sleep,
guard her till she stirred back to life
having deciphered theories
buried in the fields of her dreams
drawn from that Kingdom's conscience.

And I speak of no Kingdom in fiction.
I speak of one whose strength was sold
when gold aired its valediction.
I speak of one whose own rendition of all
called souls to come fall by its edition
and fold their cold theories written in folly.

I speak of the old kingdom of Mali

where unturned stones held in their grasps
fables that lapsed back to the start of time
fables, ladled and passed back on specific

breathing patterns, spoken to the lights
of flared lanterns on cold nights
gaining relevance in vocal flight
till entire villages were taught to recite
the metaphoric histories of ethics and life.

I speak of Mali
where stars rallied at night time
moon blue
scattering the heavens with pin pricks of light
through which like minds flew and listened
to the teachings of elders
banned from all labour.

Back there,
she had fortune's favour
now she is simply the next door neighbour.

Displaced, this Queen slaves under starless skies
in high-rise buildings and office blocks pushing
broomsticks and mops through cubicles for a living.
To ease the pain in her tired back
she packs her senses behind stacks
of sun filled memories and hums
distilled work songs
grilled under Malian suns
to match the sweep of her arm's swing.

You've seen her;
that aging woman who sings
in a strange and raspy voice
songs that have caused
the unused parts of me to gasp
and rejoice in the simple pleasure
of being alive.
Her songs are sonic hives of pain
that force me to close both eyes
and taste the bitter juice of beaten joys
slain by famine, plague and pestilence.
In the vague silence from which

    her songs reach me,
they breach the brick walls of my being;
slam like psalms through the red rocks
of my mental blocks
freeing my senses
from the false defences
of thinking that this lady is that
little bit crazy.

With my eyes closed
I start to listen
breath turns cold
reality goes that little bit hazy
and I find myself in the backwaters
of her history, painting pictures
with the perfect palette
of her words.

And she sings
of waking up one starless night
finding her household struck by a plague
bodies lying cold un-speckled un-aged;
of an unborn child caged in its dead mother's womb
desperately kicking for breath
destined for death
and not even having lived yet;
of cradling her last grandchild
giving all she had
just to reach the next morning
and find herself yawning
on a stiffened face
eyes still open, pointed to the stars
no pulse, no pace, as his soul soars
and she is left, locked behind the bars
of living, all alone;

of finally leaving her home, to a distant land
where elders are murdered for gold and money
and even in the summer
the sun shines cold.

But she lives on
bruised and bold
singing her sweet songs
so the masses hear them.

As she walks that famished road
a single thought guides her;

that when she dies
her spirit will gain that
ultimate prize and she
will live that
happily ever
after-life.

The Last Rebels

In a galaxy far, far away;
in the cradle clutch of destiny
in the arms of fate, in the bottomless
bowls of eventuality,
the beat goes on.

Through the blocked ears of walls
that have learnt not to listen
and the partings of lips
that have learnt to tell tall tales
in bare basements and brown bathrooms
the rhythm is ceaseless and no matter
how much we deny the truth
the beat goes on
and on.

The last rebels
watch the sun go down.
They watch the silent silhouettes
flint- headed censor the spotlight.
Now forced to navigate with only thought
they buy through the false theories
and re-master the muffled memories
of a time mime free.
They dine
on seasoned remnants
of history wishing to resurrect them;
but there are setbacks.

From that Galaxy,
the last rebels look
to the second continent
and see the contortion of truth
where the sick are led to believe

that raping babies
is an AIDS relief.

From that galaxy,
the last rebels look
to the western hemisphere
and witness the folly of men
where thirteen feet
from a full food disposal system
lies a half-conscious kid
who has to rest
after 13 steps
cause his body
running on empty
can't abide that stress
and he sends his sprit to syringe the stars
lest, driven hopeless
he submits to death
via collision and cars.

And worse still
the last rebels watch
as, under the guise of "epidemics"
the powers that be test out viruses
on many proletarians.
Of that many
the humanitarian few
who know the truth are silenced
so the secrets lie hidden
within rhythm of life
and the last rebels sit
knives at the ready
and watch the beat
go on.

Now what if I were to tell you
that we are The Last Rebels;
that in this galaxy it has been said

that a man-powered plague plagued recently
and we called it SARS;

would you Rise up?
Would you Riot?
Would you Rage?

Would that even make a change?
I think not.

Because at the heart of the human problem
is the problem of the human heart.

To cause these conflicts to depart
our part is to remix the rhymes that rhyme within
flip that beat and dance to a new theme;
one that doesn't falsify or cover up
causing men to die
causing men to commit suicide;
one without police brutality
bursting at the edges...
and yes

I believe in the existence of police brutality.
The fatalities of men, darker than blue
have danced through the vapours of my inkwells
have lanced through the shells of truth
their magnified absences are the fruits
and till we feed
we shall ever go hungry.

So the beat goes on
cross galaxy
the beat goes on
never knowing ever strong
the beat goes on
all knowing, all wrong
the beat goes on
the beat goes on
the beat goes on.

Babylon Battle Babble

Once upon a time
In a kingdom far, far away
it was thought that the fathers of fortune
feathered the wings of beggars and bettered
the winds of change.

It was thought that fate smiled
on those who toiled while the sun shined;
thought, that the luminary minds of men
could make the mountain range
strange to its own peak.

I speak of worlds where metaphors
were the building blocks of teachings
the sonic backdrop of songs were further reaching;
not a mis-educated, mis-vocalist's preaching
about her future husband's wallet
breaching the realms of normality
before love could reach informality.

I speak of worlds where
wars were last resorts visited in scenarios evident.
Now, bombs drop through thoughts flawed
mind power rendered irrelevant.
Distant nebulae that once nestled
in the bellies of thought streams
have been forced to stay unseen
as time stretches on.

I speak of worlds
that once spawned rock solid morals
instead of all being pawned for the dollar
and 50 Cents. Mass spasms of spondulick interference
send men claiming to be *dogs* and *cats*, path-strayed.
Because the path back to God lies

in the realization that we are just
human.

And this world is jungle.

We stand in the centre, fuming
led by snakes into the maze of thorns
thickets and Bush-es.
The time will come when we stand
beneath the solar plexus of the sun
and demand to be free
mine are the lost soliloquies of redemption songs
I hope you will stand and sing with me.

I hope you will sing
when I speak of worlds
where pro-optic stardust
layered all pupils and all souls could star
the sky, dance like metaphysical butterflies
tracing happy trails through the third age
of a global lie, exhuming the true meaning of life.

And I speak of worlds
where fathers fathered
the notion that all females flowered as queens
and from their fountains
kings would rise
planting feathers
in the shadows of their footsteps.

Mothers mothered the notion that
other than love, nothing mattered.
But paper chasing atoms have scattered
that pattern of thought, Nike's bought
the revolution, we charge through life
dodging boulders of mass confusion
like: "don't think, *Just do it*",

but mine is the chosen path through chaos;
I'll run through it.

I search for higher learning.
I am yearning to move on
but we are living in Babylon.
So I search for *Spokenword* spots
to open mike and babble on
about being here, trying
to vocally express the fears
locked in the spineless tears
of symphonies of silent souls.
These often exist
in the abyss of my own
so I battle on
trying to save myself –
once whole

I have been scattered and pattered
among the fields of everyday people
our destinies are tied together
for better or worse
I pose and prose and speak word.

And if the day comes
that these forces grow
greater than my might
I will not go gently into that good night
I will stay and fight.
Forced to the navy corners of isolation
I will ignore the call of desperation
fall to my knees and take my last breath
wielding my vocal sword's echo
till death
WORD

word
word
word
word
word
...
..

Alice in Never-Lover Land

Once upon a time
in a kingdom far away
in the thirteenth hour of night
eleven lightings after dreams come out to play
nine seconds from a kiss goodnight
for the seventh time, a little girl sits
on a floor cross-legged
flips open a book titled
"13 Fairy Negro Tales"
finds her page in five seconds
and in three moments
and two blinks
focuses on a description
of one brown woman…

"In a mountain made entirely of soil
a blue crystal was grown
and its seeds were thrown
to the sands from which oceans
and seas came forth.
"This woman's hands
were moulded by the farmer
who toiled that mountain's land.

"Her bones were crafted from Ivory
sold to the artists of the Titans
who were told to create with it
something greater than themselves.
They kept those bones
shelved them till they were
reincarnated as light
and baptised them in the unseen hues
of rainbows which solidified and became
whole, so when she moved
her shadows echoed spectrums.

"Her shoulder blades once waded in Maya
and emerged making moon ripples
on the Mesolithic rock face of ever.

"Like the ghosts of lilies
flock printed on slate
her cheeks skin-kiss
the gates of a brown heaven.
Her voice is rooted in the fantastic
flying like silk
fed on feather fractals
falling like angel zest."

And I know that woman.
We have conversed.

Many times,
I have cycled through the cities
of her psyche and left graffiti growing
on the walls her mental
making music
using palms as amplifiers
losing myself in the masts
of a friendship made to last.
And when I realised that this
between us, this might be
the stuff of greatness
I stopped.

Took a step back

tore my heart off my sleeve
and offered it to her
on a silver platter saying:
  "Lady
take this.
Wipe your soul with it.
Wear it when the winds change.
Sew it into a cushion and sleep on it
beneath the changing boughs

of the woes of the world
wear me like a breast plate
keep me like a glove, lady
let me Love you."

But she said "No,
it's far too late".

She said that in the past
she had been disappointed, failed;
that men that are not smart;
men with flawed logic
and lazy feet
climbed through the windows of her soul
to the bowels of her belly
and left seeds of weeds
that be eternally growing
eternally towing
eternally tugging
at the small saplings of beauty
left in her heart, and *she would not*
she could not start nothing with no one;
there was no place for love
none.

None.

And that
    left me lost ...
  in the winter
of her solitude
caught in a courtyard
of dying roses and
dead crystals
with one pen to coat me
from the cold.

One pen.

So with that pen

I am painting a new portrait.

It is of a man, who sculpts crystals for a living
whose pupils are calibrated
to reflect that woman's own
whose hugs mimic Maya
who is wiling to be the earth for her to grow on
and be cherished; a man to replenish.

And when this portrait is finished
when it is nailed to parchment
I shall mail it to the mystics
hoping that they cast it into living
hoping that fate comes around to my way
of seeing and makes him be
so he can live *her* for me
so he can love her
for me
for that is what poets do

we dream.

we dream
in the thirteenth hour of night
eleven lightings after playtime
nine seconds before a kiss goodnight,
before a little girl closes a book of tales…

leans back to sleep, leaving a *bag lady* locked
in the pages of an experience;
me half empty; both
subconsciously wishing for

happily
ever
after.

The One About God

In a galaxy far, far away
in the grand canyons
of an afro-hued wilderness
before the naturally formed
symbol of fertility; raised from rock
born of wind and wisdom, locked
to the uncontrolled, uncorked
gateway to all worlds and all words;
to the left of a camp fire fuelled
by wooden swords; sits a purple man
with sky blue pupils and sand dusted hands.

In his left hand, he holds 3.6 cowry shells
2 pens, one scroll times infinity.
In his right, he holds a mic, which he raises
to his lips, turns to face the north and speaks:

"I have seen God! "
"Last week, he walked like Osiris.
He was last seen selling incense sticks
to girls on street corners. The day before
he sat mourning his bullet-battered friend -
another black man turned to dust.
Despite the heartache and the rust
the next day, with his emotions
nailed to his sleeve and his spirit lost
he was back at that street corner
barely standing on his feet
still selling".

Saying this, old man turns
to the eastern world and whispers:

"I have seen God,
at the tender age of six,

kidnapped from his family,
assigned a bed of bricks, 3 bullets,
one gun and five rebel songs, he was
bullied into battle and forced to partake
in random scores of killing.
As fortune would have it, he was captured
dropped on a landmine and left lower limb-less,
yet in anti-war rallies
you can hear his voice
preaching peace".

Saying this he turns
to the south and says to the southern wind:

"I have seen God.
She walks with death.
She was informed she had terminal
cancer and a few months to live. Today
5 years later, she runs marathons to raise funds
to research and combat that cancerous killing.
In spite of that ever tightening
noose towards her last hour
she refuses to cower with fright;
she stands and fights".

And with the wind speed rising
shadows and silhouettes flying
to welcome the night, this purple
man turns to the western word and bellows to the dying light;

"I HAVE SEEN GOD!
she was disguised as Shawana
a single mother. She rocks two jobs
three kids, two cars and gives change to homeless
others. She can go from corporate to ghetto
she rocks red stilettos with earth brown badus
and has cowry shells laced
to her laptop carry-case."

With that, he vanished into nothingness

but his last blue breath said this:

"We spend so much time looking to heaven
that we put ourselves through hell.
We ignore the daily miracles that line our streets
looking for supernatural signs that God exists
when it is written: *God exists within us*

This is found everywhere:
in the diaries of Shamen. Found
in the log books of logarithms
doodled on the petals of each rose
that grows from rock; it is hidden
in the souls of sell-outs
sprinkled on the sands
of time; it is stamped
on the palms of check-out girls
paying their way through college
and 90 year old dreads
still seeking knowledge;
it is paraphrased from Biblic verses
versed in Quranic lines;
it is found in rap
rhythm and rhyme
it is bared on the conquered
mountain of Everest
it is now left for y'all to take,
rest and be as
happily, ever, after
as you can.

Brother's Keeper Person Thing

Once upon a time,
there lived a man.
Born to the speech patterns
of street slang, he was raised
to the ever present sounds of sirens
wailing through the effervescent
failing lights of a brick-city estate

Fatherless from birth
he modelled himself on thugs
stole and dealt drugs, then caught
and convicted, he was locked
in lone confinement.

In the silence that followed
he saw himself- whole.
The desolation seen
sowed a new him.
So, released, he went straight
and fortune reads:
he reaped the fruits of seeds sewn pure.
But beyond the shores
of this paradise clouds loomed.

His colleagues hated the thought
of *the great unwashed* rising
through suds, clean and glistening
so they bowed their heads together
eyebrows furrowed, nostrils flared
nose hairs bristling
and plotted the fall of a man
who gave his all.

And in this same kingdom

there lived a woman.
Made to leave school
at sweet sixteen
she was forced-married to a fool
who raped her every night
till her self confidence and might
were crucified to the sounds
of her tears.
Her fears took flight
when she found a new soul
growing inside her
but her husband hit harder
and left her on her own
16 years old, pregnant
dishonored, disowned.

Like this she lived
in hostels and shacks
spirit cracked
baby strapped to her back
raiding dustbins for food
addicted to smack
to mask her life's hell

and now she sells sex,
son by her side
spirit hovering beyond reach
contemplating suicide.

And these two stories, these people
do not live far and wide
they are your friend's neighbour
your sister's old boss
the silently sitting sigh-ers on a bus.
Find them
the faceless fellows
praying in whispered bellows
that their tragedies be lightened
by human touch.

So if you see that man walking
with his spirit on a crutch
or that specific sister
raving about giving up…

If you see them

tell them I have their dreams.

Tell them I have their dreams.
Tell them that they're planted in a new age
blue festering through Aquarius, a new stage.
Tell them that that I have turned the page and
inscribed with glowing white ink
their names on the pages of tomorrow.
Tell them that hope has burrowed through their lands
and laid eggs in their earth-sands and there is a new birth
beyond the bands of that dark night.
Tell them I have seen their spotlight
and it is love-shaded.
Tell them that their storms have been sedated
by the whispered words of a bellow's exhaled
echoed last breath
for nothing lasts for ever;
even fires succumb to death.

Tell them it's always darkest before
a sunburst's first zest.

Tell them to take it easy.
Tell them to rest.

Tell them to picture the pressed
warm juices of a soft stream
no haste.
Tell them to savour those seconds.
Tell them to taste.
Tell them fortune comes to those who wait.
I have heard their futures,
their laughter rings true.

Tell them their skies are blue.
Tell them they lived
happily ever after.

Tell them that it's true.

The Last Bohemian

In a galaxy far away,
adjacent to burnt sienna sunrises and Starbucks
symbols that hover just over
forbidden land.

Hidden
behind the buildings forged
to cage thought;
echoing images of freedom un-bought
to a background of melanin music;
wrought of men that be telling what truth is,
overlooking stacks of de-framed
photographs of ol' Blue Eyes
singing *I did it my way*;
on a cliff
graffitied with colours
once imprisoned in a prism;
risen from earth and *don't-be-different* dissing;
caught in a cloud of conformity
is the dwelling place of the last bohemian.

It is a heaven for all things 'one',
a five leaf clover, a purple sun
a peeling diamond, a bullet ridden gun
a disco ball spitting sultry songs of solitude
a tube of H2O un-passed through human body
un pushed through human flesh, a painting of a Neo-
shaman moulding ocean lingo
a potion to poster a riff's row
a feline felon's forgotten flow
the recorded bellow of a new age fellow
a red mist faded yellow
a mellow-melanin-man, a first stand
a captured moment of light glinting on chrome
a shape in static, a monochrome-matic necklace

of green olives, seeds and pollen
a falling tree in a silence's constant
a constant red line with a blue period

for only through periods of constants,
is the need for change made apparent.
And the apparent parents the change in turn.
The last bohemian embodies that all:

A feather caught in a cyclone
whirl winded into the iris of a prayer
sent from a prairie, palm-kissed into existence.
A red flare in the pacific blue
a pacifist in true danger
a water baby in a sand castle
a rhythm ranger
a birth in a manger,
the metal matter of Excalibur unmade
a firefly dazzling with shade
a linen cloth on silk,
a black eyed pea floating in milk
a Griot gloating at a broken memory chip
a weather butterfly woken to walk the walk
for they that only talked the talk
a cross hatch in a gradient
a remedy in a realm of ailments
a hot rock in heaven, a hailstone in hell
a fairy negro tale teller in the land of myths and legends
a reject, registered as reverting back to one
a blue wire in a red storm, a torn sheet showing
children of the corn, chanting
"no change, no progress"

And the last bohemian be the body of progress
for the last bohemian be the body of change
and the last bohemian bears the power of birth
for the last bohemian…
is a woman.

Men are just not metal enough.

Her daughters will dance the death of revolutions
and give birth to new ones to take their place.
They will write this story before it is too late
they will live
happily
ever
after

Dustbin Diaries

Once
upon a time,
a young man gleaned
from an archaic continent creamed
in the light fantastic;
from the borders of history baked
before an African sun
came to this kingdom
of Babylon.

This kingdom became his home.
And as time turned its page
suit followed his age –
this now withered warrior
is whom I see before me.

The way he sits shows
that his toes were once kissed
by born again rain dancers.
You can read the wisdom
in his posture, you can taste it.
With his back straight
face forward, shoulders broad
you can tell that he was made to lord over many;
you can sense the toasts of the past, those-loyal-to-life
casting coats his way.
The dustbin he sits on wears
the ghost formation of a throne cast in light
shown only if you squint with your third eye
and let ether-light loan itself to the moment.

History is grooved in his garments.
The heaviness drags his movements
as chains clink on his collar.
The Mississippi that burns on his right shoulder

is dowsed with the water ways
of Saro Wiwa on his left.
The pride of escaped slaves rises from them
like the steam created when magma hits seawater.
The zest of greatness rests on his chest
gracing all that is he, intoxicating all that is me
culminating in his presence growing, dignity glowing
seven inches past his torn and tattered clothes.

But in the wake of all this glory,
I sense his light dimming towards its close.

So I wish.
I wish for a star studded tobacco leaf
filled with newly made mortal matter
meaning for him to smoke it
and defer the coming of the last latter
so he may live longer
but all that I reap is the wind.

Instead
I reach into my pocket
and retract a handful of me
disguised as silver coins
and drop it into the empty coffee cup
beside him "Sir", I whisper, foolishly
trying to use those coins as payment
to the pastures of his spirit. "Sir", I say
once again, expecting to gain entrance
to the campsites of his soul, "Sir, Old
man, how did it get to be like this?"

Silence.

In the empty seconds that follow
He is still. Like a gathering of mango
farmers awaiting the moon rise
or children, breaths held
awaiting the Griot's first message

like a choir of pencils
waiting to chorus words
or wash women of the Nile
awaiting Cleopatra's descent
He is still.

Then he stirs.

He stirs like a mountain
streaked with silver dread locks
like a black tide coming in
commanding time to witness
one of its many prodigal sons
he stares and says…

"Son,
the world just ain't big enough no more.
We have devalued the mystery of life
for the values of materialistic living
I am from a time when whole villages mourned
our passing, and now the masses complain
that we live too long.

Son, I am past my die-by date.
These silver pieces of your soul means
that I shall marvel at the moon once more
but it is far too late, move on son
you can do no more.
Just take with you this truth,
we are the 'yous' of yesterday.
You will become the 'wes' of tomorrow.
If you do not wish to live on a trash can like this
then you must walk in our shoes today."

The silence after he speaks
is stone aged.

I walk gently into the night,
thankful to have been kissed
with a vital catalyst

for living happily
ever
after.

Swahilian Gingerbread Men

A long ago time in this kingdom
key holes were more than gateways
granting entrance to the other side.

Pebbles were much more
than rebel ambassadors of a rock
face and the powers that letters wore
yielded much more than messages.

Around each square moment of existence
mysteries were littered like lilies in snow.
Since then
the winters have grown wilder
but those white whispers are still
peeking through the snow
and if you haven't seen them
yet, someday you will see them too.

In the cracks of pavements
you will see them;

Armies of Swahilian gingerbread men
sipping opium water
and lemon drops
licking the last cranberry crystal crops
off the backs of blue lady bugs
begging them to once again dictate
the story of ever.

You will hear them
choirs of Celtic b-boys
rocking Scottish kilts
creating soft-rock-reggae
in an old railway station
radiating reason to recess

with their voices receding down hallways
and their echoes returning
always
always
always….

You will smell them
the fragrance of forgotten forefathers
and the faded fractals of fauna found
on the windowsills to wisdom
and in the spines of books.

You will see them
serenaded in sunrise
testimonials of young time tellers
dressed in graffiti's form trailing truth
through multi toned tears, tagged
onto the tapestry of concrete
stapled to yesterday
today and tomorrow.

Like
right now
in a secret garden
guarded by green angels
there is an ancient fruit bearing tree
holding the oldest love letter
carved in its bark
enclosed in
its heart
reading;

Adam 'n' Eve 4 eva

Born
on the same day
as infinity, these are part of the endless
mysteries that litter our daily lives

and if you haven't seen them

yet, someday, you will see them too.

In the citadel of a second
2 nano-moments from now
eleventeen blinks from the next *whenever*
a benevolent eloquent elephant
tipsy on musk, will bow to deer pressure
and donate his tusks to charity.

A leprechaun lost
in solid gold raking
will start gold-baking begonia battered
broomsticks to sweep every residence
where poetry be president
and every man listening
will start clapping,
and the minute after that,
nothing will have happened.

See…
the next minute is as much a mystery
as the mystery that dwells within the *minute*
and that *minute* minute of mystery stretches
far.

It covers empty envelopes marked "top secret".
It is laughter wafting after the day goes down.
It is a poet extracting Iranian juice from a memory
and posing, metaphysically, a prose with its juice.
It is a shadow cut loose.

It is how wind flows through water
awakening wonder in the womb of seeds
vibrating to trees, off springing clouds
that wring water back to wind which whistles
where ever the weather goes…

It is a barefooted, newly born
Nubian, new-being bohemian
in an urban basement, baby-bashing

beats on an upturned wooden basin,
bearing a rhythm older than his own father's
wisdom and not knowing where it came from
just ad-libbing to it in baby speech form.

These mysteries line our streets
and in their midst, I sit
on a mountain top
with my Iranian scented ink
trace words on winds
sink to blue worlds
drink nectar
and think…

  and
    think.

about Jacob Sam-La Rose

Jacob Sam-La Rose's poetry has been characterised as vivid, masterly and carefully structured. He is widely recognised as an indefatigable facilitator, mentor and supporter of young and emerging poets, and as an advocate for the positive impact of new technology on literary and artistic practice and collaboration. His debut pamphlet, Communion (2006), was a Poetry Book Society Pamphlet Choice and his collection Breaking Silence (2012) was shortlisted for both a Forward Poetry Prize (the Felix Dennis Award) and the 2012 Fenton Aldeburgh Award.

author statement

Putting the pamphlet together was relatively painless. That was due in part to the fact that the pamphlet was mostly comprised of pieces I was already quite familiar with, poems that had been worked over an extended period of time; but also to Nii's unforgiving yet relaxed editorial eye. The process was entirely alive to and responsive to my poetics, and served to bring the best out of my writing, rather than mould me to fit some other accepted or recognised stance. The poems came together in a way that simply felt right, and the editing offered that intuitive grouping and ordering the polish and sharpening it needed.

kudos

winner of
Poetry Book Society Pamphlet Choice (2006)
shortlisted for
Forward Poetry Prize - Felix Dennis Award (2012)
Fenton Aldeburgh Award (2012)

Communion

COMMUNION

Jacob Sam-La Rose

First Published: 2006
Series Number: 03
Editor: Nii Ayikwei Parkes

Communion

Why?

The sound of a letter.

The greatest question, reducing sense
to its smallest indivisible fraction.

A battering ram.

The finest indefatigable blade.
A skeleton key. A house breaker.
Sometimes an ending in itself.

Everything you want it to be.

A Crowd of Sounds

My Mother's Guitar

*"Between my finger and my thumb
The squat pen rests; snug as gun."*
- Digging, Seamus Heaney

Hefting its weight for the first time in years,
wiping the dust from its curves, I want to know
if her mother ever sang to her
the way she sang to me. I was made

for those evenings, cross-legged at her feet,
listening close to each song, strings
chirping against her fingers,
its wide hips notched on her thigh.

Some nights she'd perch on the edge
of her bed, hands crabbed around its neck
and together they'd sing, pulling
thick-throated notes from thin air,

more magic than television. Did her mother
place those melodies under her tongue,
keepsakes to pass down, proof against
the fear of being forgotten? She stopped;

I don't remember when or why,
and I wish I'd learned to play, to hold
the chords she held, catch something of her
voice. The keys turn easily,

tightening the strings back into life
but my fingers don't know how to make
her music. Instead, I write it all down.

Bacchanal

Carnival nights, it was all too easy
    to be caught by the current: a river
        of bodies that flooded the streets,
    anchored to the sounds of floats

loaded with man-sized black boxes,
    monuments to sound, speakers
        whose hearts crackled and snapped,
    near broken with the weight of their own bass.

If you could work through the crush, press
    your hands against a grille, the music would
        breathe on you, itch the air around your fingers
    ring your chest like a gong.

I'd watch from the side, eager
    but too shy to learn the language
        they spoke: the hips and thighs.
    They had their own rolling rhythms,

fluid, fierce and independent.
    The boys I walked with called themselves
        the man dem; had their own brand
    of manners, would almost never ask.

At best, they'd dive headlong
    into that tide, surface and press
        the whisper of a quick hot smile
    up close behind an ear,

behind slicked down curls or pressed hair
       pulled tight to escape the heat.
              Quick hands, snaking around waists,
       pulling themselves forward,

searching for a rhythm to hold
       steady as rock.

Sound

Bright toothed smiles, firefly cigarette butts
and the low, rude lick of a bass line.

Teenage, me and the rest of the boys,
moving through the thick air

of a darkened room, each of us, peeling off
on our own in search of a sticky heat,

drawn by the kinds of moments that bind
couples in dark corners for the length

and breadth of a song. There's one.
One woman, standing alone,

somehow separate from the crush.
Her feet anchored, waistline rolling

as if caught in the swell of some high tide,
the heel of an upturned palm at her temple.

I can imagine a dark wet shadow
pooling in the small of her back

where I'd place my hand having asked her
to dance and learn to match her rhythm,

a rhythm that, even now, across the room
dares me to approach, and yet,

watching, I think I understand
this music, this deep-rooted sound,

how its palpable tremor becomes
her perfect partner.

After Lazerdrome: McDonalds, Peckham Rye...

*"What's clear, now, is / that there was music, that it's lasted, that
it / doesn't matter whether a player played it, / or whether it just
played itself, that it still is / playing, / that at least two gods exist..."*
- from 'A Dispute About God', Abdulah Sidran

where I say goodbye to south-east London for the next 3 years
a gaggle of us   still damp   spilling in from the night before

early flock for a Sunday   six or seven a.m.   sleepless
drowning in light and all this quiet   after all that sweat
and darkness   all that flighty noise

this is the year one of the guys says music is the one thing
that won't ever let him down   that music is his religion

the year we're stopped and searched because we
fit the description   the year jungle music passes
out of fashion   stripped down

to naked beat and bass   and we club together   to dance
alone   in the dark   let the music play us   meat and bone

let music fill the empty spaces   rhythm in wads and scads
scattershot   crashing   wall to wall   to be baptised
by filtered drums   pressed snares and swollen b-lines

be baptised by city songs   urban hymns   seamless
sound   a brimming sea of sound   poured out

from towering speaker stacks   this is the year we stand
close enough   to feel the music   rise   its wing-beats
on our faces   drawing salt from our skin   released

then morning   small fries and a strawberry milkshake
counting coins for the cab back   sitting around a table

slouching in moulded seats   drowning in silence
light-headed   leavened   waiting
for the right moment to move

awake for too long   ears
still ringing   drum-drunk

eyes still adjusting to the light
a weight coming down

The Faithful

In my family, church on a Sunday morning was never a matter of choice.
I didn't know any arguments that might rescue me from the stiff routine
of a starched shirt and neatly seamed strides. Didn't know any prayers.
Knew better than to try.

The reverend towered in the pulpit, a flushed neck throttled by the
contrast of a pure white collar. He spat sermon into the vaults of echoing
empty air above the heads of the congregation. I figured he was selling
after-life insurance for the price of a Sunday morning subscription, a sip of
the blood, which was given, and wafer of bleached, celestial flesh.

Take, eat, this is the body...

It seemed enough to sit there. Daydream. Think of the Sunday morning
re-runs of Saturday morning cartoons I was missing. Wonder if it was
true that God could see through thoughts like the x-ray specs advertised
in the back of every comic book; if it was true that God knew what
everyone was thinking, even the thoughts of those few people sleeping in
the pews, eyes closed as if marking the passing parables deep in prayer,
heads nodding off-beat, almost as if they could hear every word...

On a good day, the sun would stream in through the stained glass,
catch the metal of the watch on my wrist and dance a wild, flickering
shine across the high, arched ceiling. A shine that, sometimes, became a
spotlight, subtle as the gaze of God may possibly have been, if God was
ever there, searching for the faces of the faithful.

Never

He never taught me how to hold
a pair of clippers. I never saw him
dab cologne on his cheeks. I don't know
the smell of his sweat, or if our fingers
look alike. I didn't learn to drink
by draining whatever wine he might have left
or sharing an ice cold can. He never
wrestled me down, so I never grew up
to return the favour. I didn't learn to love
music thumbing through his vinyl LPs.
I never woke him. He never once raised
his voice at me. I never heard him laugh,
and although I remember him at the end
of a long distance call, once,
I don't remember his voice,
or what it might have sounded like
saying my name.

Communion

"Make the music with your mouth, Biz!"
- Biz Markie

Street corner spotlights, cupped hands,
spit-crossed palms: solid air pressed
through teeth and lips into high-hats,
kicks, snares and even bass; the moment
passed round like a chalice or smoke,
and riding it all, always, someone
with a need to be heard.

The Spalding Suite

i. Gravity

When we were young, we worshipped stars.

Our symbols of faith were ticks and stripes
endorsed by gleaming long-limbed gods
frozen/framed in the act of impossible flight,
plastered on our walls. For a time we tried
to follow, find the staircase, learn the trick,
to rise, to carve out our own piece of sky
with a butter-smooth arc of an arm
and a Spalding ball glued to the fingertips.
We thought we knew. Sooner or later,
for each of us, gravity came calling
to shackle our ankles and dreams.

But, for a time, we were free.

ii. Again

For a summer, there was only one dream.
We flapped around a court in Shooters Hill,
flanked by tower blocks and the slim figures
of lamp-posts until the light turned soft and bad,
vests cooling where the sweat bled through.
A currency of muscle and finger tips, each of us

hustling hard to earn the calves and inches
needed to break past hand-checks and other
outstretched palms; learning to cover a baseline,
to dance and shuck, make and break
a rhythm of ball and bounce,

hit a bone-hard screen and stay
upright, to palm a ball, still singing
from it's last bounce, and hoist it
like a prayer, all the way to the rim –

an open mouth, responding to everything
with the same silent answer.
Again, it said.

Do it
again.

A rectangle of tarmac. Your slender fingers
and ripening biceps find purpose.

      Your wings unfurl, shake loose.

You're learning to time your steps, find
an angle of ascent that allows you to

      pause the reel,

hold a heartbeat, draw it out
like a heartfelt sigh.

      All you want

is for someone to give you
the gift of your name on the back of

      an awed breath,

but the tarmac is teeming with others,
each with his own brand of magic.

      The ground

is littered with feathers.
You jostle for air.

iv. Beauty

New Cross. We found a court on a backstreet, hungry
for new ground, eager to test our game against
no one we really knew. Not that any of us

was ever that good. Under a pestle of mid-day sun,
one kid cut through us with a crossover fade, smooth
as any girl's pressed hair. Two steps, up and away,

kissing the ball with his fingers, feeding it through
the hoop. Few things I remember as beautiful.
We stopped, hands on hips, faces twisted

from the effort of trying to keep up, to stop him
from rising. The distance brayed. He belonged
to the air, something we were trying to be,

brought it close enough to touch, and passed us, again
and again. We praised him with a chorus of ragged breath.
Him, already pulling the ball back for the next play.

v. The Brothers of Ladywell Fields

To me, they look like angels, brazen
as broad daylight. I used to run with them,

and I'll tell you the truth: girls never gathered
to watch us swagger or swoop to the rim.

We played for the love of rising
above each other, inhabiting

all that empty air, connecting each step
into nothing with a sure and hard return.

Now, my heartbeat confesses –
I'm vulnerable. My feet stutter

on the tarmac. Maybe the brothers
can read my steps, smell a fall

rising from my skin like sweat.
I know too well the raucous clang

of a near miss on the rim, the way
a smooth arc can turn ugly at the end,

and all that air still remains.
Perhaps I was closer to god.

I haven't held the ball like that
for years.

Clockwork

Brittle

I was always a serious child.
I never believed

that a lost tooth, buried
under a pillow and a wish

could be resurrected
as some dream come true.

I knew it would be there,
each morning, still

the same small nugget
of dirty pearl,

crusted in blood,
evermore brittle.

The Hours

My other father - the one that stayed - worked nights when I was a
kid. I've never understood nightshifts, although I've pulled them since,
making my business while everything else rests; never understood the
way the sun comes up like laughter over your shoulder, some private joke.
Lonely hours, home to all the essential undesirable occupations that keep
the world ticking over, push it through into another day. He drove a mail
truck up and down the country and always came back at four or five in
the morning - hours I was only dimly aware of, hours my body passed
through in sleep, like ghost towns between cities. At first, I slept light,
woken by the sound of his key in the lock, a foreign thing. Soon, I learned
to sleep through. Some nights I woke when his feet took the stairs, slow,
with care, so as to keep the hour sacred, undisturbed.

Algebra

For OPRF High School, Chicago

I'm 29 in a high school maths lesson.
I've had dreams like this. Nightmares.

The teacher speaks a different language,
a vocabulary of numbers. Inconsistent graphs.
Tests. Slopes. $x+y$. $y=3x-2$. I daydream that

maybe there's music in these numbers.
If x were a tree and y were a sound,
negative a over b might =

the Chicagoan wind, a fiddlestick of air
making leaves sing. I imagine black notes
rolling down a woman's cheek.

Last night, I saw a woman cry,
stunned by the strength of her own words
scored on a page, a flood of memory.

There are numbers everywhere.
The teacher gives two methods of solving
equations: substitution or elimination.

The woman that cried has three siblings.
She, the only one that kept her mother's Xmas bow.
She hasn't seen her mother for seven months.

Immigration = a blank wall with no doors,
dividing her family, crowned by an eagle
looking down from a nest of barbed wire.

The teacher points to the board and asks
is this consistent? A student asks if this is the point
of intersection. The woman that shed tears

doesn't know if she'll see her mother again,
and there's a music in everything: in chalk
tapping out problems and solutions on a board,

in layers of chalk dust falling on a classroom floor
like passing minutes, in school bells marking
a lesson's end, in tears coaxed into words.

And where there's music, there's beauty.

Pendulum

The girl on front desk in reception will probably keep the baby.
The boy in the office behind her doesn't know what to do.
One night, after hours, you sit on a cold brick wall,
your arm around her shoulders, holding her together
as the tears come too suddenly for her to speak
and she cries into her palms, too weak to stand.
You want to help. He's not there. She calls it love.

It's beginning to rain as it often does in movies
at moments like this, and you don't know it yet,
but there will be phone calls. She will drag you out of sleep,
her voice blurred with questions. Hours will pass.
Some nights, the way she describes him will chime
with the shadows chased across your wall by passing headlights.
Days from now, she will show you his picture in her wallet, back
behind the plastic with other important things, smiling
as if he never left. It will dizzy you.

You will learn to guarantee that nothing stays the same,
that everything moves. You will remember a physics lesson,
a teacher that spoke of constant flux. A pendulum's swinging weight.
But you won't be able to find any way to stop that pendulum's
back and forth, any more than you could stop
one minute bleeding into the next.
The best you can do, now, is hold her close,
and strain to hear, somewhere deep inside her,
a different clock beginning to mark it's own time.

Clockwork

Shadows come to power - night
settles in. An absence of light
defied by streetlamps and signage.

The window is closed, every sound
silenced by the soft-edged stench
of bleach, mopped floors and sterile sheets.

Then, in her sleep, she turns. He unlocks
his fingers from hers. Moves to pull
the curtains. He wants to press his face

against the glass, feel a cold shock
blaze across his cheek, watch his breath
mist and spread, some important part of him,

visible in front of the world. Outside,
there's still the clockwork of taillights,
and above, travelling inexorably,

the hulking forms of clouds,
the blind weight of all that air.

Autumn

i.

...and the sun's light is a bleached smear on a soiled rag. Anything ever pinned to the sky must finally kiss the ground. Leaves, bruised by brighter days, fall like plucked feathers. Trees flame until they bare themselves against an ashen sky; spent, bleeding into the colours of used pennies, they'll never burn this way again.

ii.

She left. Plain and simple. He imagines himself a room, void of furniture, empty and cavernous, light bleeding in through flat grey slats. No heat in the air; water waiting silent and solid in the pipes. Her laughter echoes from the walls. The sound of her voice settles like dust on the hardwood floor.

Seconds

Anything past the horizon / is invisible, it can only be imagined. You want to see the future but / you only see the sky.
- Road Music, Richard Siken

Late night, flicking through stations on the car stereo
you tune in on a rasping voice, hoisted
over lilting acoustic chords; a song
you've never heard before. The road opens
in front of you, and there's nothing about this song
you don't already know, even down to the rasp,

the way the voice is honeyed with heartache,
the rough edge calculated to sound raw
and real. Every note is second hand.
And maybe there's some other place you need to be.
Somewhere else, where something is happening,
without you, now, something so vital

that it calls out from wherever it is,
and you don't know how to get there.
Maybe you're not driving. Maybe you're trying
to put words down on a blindingly blank page.
Maybe you're trying to get dressed.
Or maybe your hands are resting lightly

on the back of the neck of the person
you're supposed to love now,
and maybe, for a moment,
you can't tell the difference
between that neck
and any other neck you've known.

Aubade

Waking, you find yourself on a balcony, hands clasped over the edge, forearms resting too hard on the cool black railing. A room falling back into shadow through the open door behind you. You never thought it would be so easy to push back the arm that lay across you, skin sticking to the skin. To rise without a pause to wonder whether the empty impression you'd leave would be noticed, the shadow on the mattress, testament to where you'd spent the night.

Waking, you run your tongue over your teeth. Lick the salt from your lips. Spit. Crane forward to see it fall. Your eyes unsure of what to do with all the silence. Every other window in the opposite block curtained and closed. No movement in the sunrise. No distant hush of traffic. No song. Nothing, except the dark shape of a body stood by a stoplight on the corner below. The dark shape of a man, his face turned up towards you, so still he could be chiselled stone, sculpted. So still that he belongs to this morning, to the cars parked and driverless and the shadows clinging to the ground beneath them.

You perch there, hands clasped over the edge, looking down at him. Realising he may not see you. Maybe he, too, is looking for something in the pinks and blues of this half-lit morning sky. Maybe he, like you, wonders how long this moment can last. Maybe there's a woman in a room behind him that will wake soon, reach out and feel him gone. And regardless of whether he sees you or not, you raise a hand to your head in mock salute. Knowing that he, like you, is simply waiting. Waiting to see how long it will be before something, again, begins to move. Waiting to see what happens next.

Freedom

To write this, I remember a night too hot
to sleep – a night on which the single window
refused to shift, and the room sweltered.

That night, I dragged myself downstairs,
jealous of the child my cousin used to be,

his talent for hard sleep. In sleep, his body
danced, loose, unguarded, trying to find
a shape it felt it fit, willing to walk the corridor

to the front room, where you'd find him
next morning, face down on the couch, slender

fingers trailing on the floor, him oblivious
and innocent, asking who'd moved him in the night.
Now he's grown. Grown into a world

in which even sleep is scrutinised, a bed that's not
his own, a hankering for home-cooked food.

He serves a time defined by walls. Wardens.
Wishes. If I could, I'd wish him back.
I'd wish him home, and I'd watch over him again

as he sleeps. The shapes his body takes,
and what they say of freedom.

about Truth Thomas

Truth Thomas is a singer-songwriter and poet, born in Knoxville, Tennessee and raised in Washington, DC. He studied creative writing at Howard University under Dr. Tony Medina and earned his MFA in poetry at New England College. His collections include Party of Black, A Day of Presence, Bottle of Life, finalist for the People's Book Prize in London and Speak Water, winner of the 2013 NAACP Image Award for Outstanding Literary Work in Poetry. His poems have appeared in over 100 publications, including The 100 Best African American Poems (edited by Nikki Giovanni), and been twice nominated for a Pushcart Prize.

author statement

It was an honor to have my debut pamphlet, Party of Black, published under the mouthmark series. It was an even greater privilege to have Nii Ayikwei Parkes as an editor in that process. In a very real sense, Parkes and flipped eye put me on the world stage as a writer. I count that as no small blessing—especially for a black poet. Publishing opportunities for all writers are narrow, at best. For writers of color—who often write about issues of social justice, as I do—those opportunities are slimmer still. The most important benefit of having a book published by flipped eye was that it allowed me to express myself freely in an imprint of quality. Freedom matters, for anyone—and for any poet—as does the production of finely crafted work.

kudos
winner of
NAACP Image Award for Outstanding Literary Work in Poetry
(2013)
finalist for
the People's Book Prize (2011)
included in
100 Best African American Poems (2010)

Party of Black

PARTY
OF BLACK

Truth Thomas

First Published: 2006
Series Number: 05
Editor: Nii Ayikwei Parkes

Party of Black

The I Be Tree

I be
pirate prints
on African fingers.
I be slave and Cherokee.
I be Ben Hur Ave and
Strawberry Plains, a colored
only survivor. I be Avon Nyanza,
Carrie Bell Cole, I be Five Points,
clothespins and Knoxville. I be
Mamaw and Papaw, Grandfather
Erskin, shoeshines on Central and Vine.
I be son of Carridella– who shouldn't have
made it past 3– pneumonia, paralysis, fever
and tears. I be prayers hanging over a crib.
I be Seven Day Episcopal Baptist Holiness
AME. I be segregated popcorn dropped in
Gay Street movie seats. I be picture frames for
fathers. I be women raising men. I be Mother
Macklin's crackling bread, her bat catchin rats in
the pantry. I be uncles fightin Klansmen, giving as
good as they got. I be package stores and cigarettes,
holy birds and hymnals. I be hound dogs yawning
porches. I be lightnin bugs in jars. I be trailers tied
to bumpers. I be U Hauled to DC. I be battling out on
Eastern Ave. I be afro picks with fists. I be rent strikes,
roaches, PF Flyers, James Brown on "the one." I be tank
treads rolling, U Street smoking, Corretta's assassinated smile.
I be bruises like plums on my mother's arms– a gift from my
second non-father. I be nails in his cheeks, teeth in his back,
as she gave as good as she got. I be the panther
in her eyes that stopped the attacks.
Yes
I be
all that.

Cool

(afterEthelbert)

Rock Creek Baptist Church
8th & Upshur Street, NW
Washington, DC

Reverend Hill Holy Ghosted good news in my dome
while Deacon Webster– voice bigger than the building
sang of sparrows & God's eye on them.

16 then, I wondered where the other men were. So I
asked the all knowing one– the one who healed the sick–
who made a way out of no way. I asked my mother.

And she said, "Son, it's all about the cool, and for most
men, it's just not cool to love– like Tatum loved Steinway–
like Ali loved shuffle– like Carver loved nuts–

for most men, it's just not cool to pave community over
dice, when they would rather stuff red light drawers
with dollar bills. Yes son, the reason you don't see

more men in church
is because cool
has killed them."

Soup is Good Food

Will they remember if I fed them
from my left hand or my right–

when lions growl from infant bellies
and hunger holds her trembling plate?

I've never met a doctrine
more filling than soup.

Will they remember if I fed them
or the speeches of my spoon?

Swept Away

"I held her hand as tight as I could, but she told me, 'You can't hold me.' "
- Hardy Jackson, BILOXI, Miss, one day after Katrina

The house split. I couldn't hold on– but I remember
hands
catnip
for
kisses
hands
pillows
for
prayer
hands
The house split. I couldn't hold on– but I remember

The poem above is in a new form by Truth Thomas called the "Skinny"; an 11-line form poem, where the first and last lines are the same, and are the only lines in the poem that can have more than one word. The 2nd, 6th, and 10th lines are also identical.

If They Were White

Bush would suck floodwater like an addict's last line of coke
healthcare would part the Mississippi

pillows would fall from Superdome skies as Condoleeza Rice
played Clair de lune.

If they were white, Pat Robertson would call for
Michael Brown's assassination

Re-fugees would mean good Hip Hop, looter-hungry cameras
would starve.

If they were white– at the slightest breeze, steaks
would land like C-130s

porta-potties would shine like Louis Armstrong solos, rescue
would cum quicker than a twenty dollar trick.

If they were white, aid would cling to Ninth Ward doors
like plaque sticks to Dick Cheney's veins

evacuation buses would offer deep tissue massage
bayou would turn to wine

Katrina would be another word
for Mardi Gras.

Kanye Was Right

even dogs know

which is why

they pee

on Bushes.

By Any Other Name

DoD Confirmation List: Latest Coalition Fatality: July 26, 2006
U.S. Deaths Confirmed By The DoD: 2570

Beware of

        parlor

generals

        who call

cheesewiz

        brie

crackers

        hors d'oeuvres

war

        theater.

There is No Fried Chicken in Heaven

(afterGeraldStern)

In all these bank glass pawn shops
in all this wounded hardware
I have never seen a broader bottomed boom box
nor heard Kirk Franklin spin the way I did
at the annual Martin Luther King Community Church picnic
as summer steamed with candied sweets and collards
nor slapped my knees to laughter quite as hard as I did then
so long I thought my heart would explode, playing the dozens
and dancing dominoes–in 2006–in Washington DC
home of Go Go and mosquitoes with a work ethic
6,000 miles away from that other picnic–God of mercy
oh taming God–where red was the only color spilling
over punchbowls in Iraq.

10thGraderSpeak on Prevention

(OverlisteningUStreet/Cardozo)

Okay, if she fine right, most of the time
you ain't got to worry bout catchin no
HIV. Feel me?

That's what my brotha say & he should know
cause he got mad shorties & he only a
year older than me.

He say, the best way to tell if somebody clean
is if they face is like flowers & they got
springs in they hips like Beyonce

cause he say, nobody that look like Beyonce
could make you sick. KnowhatI'msayin?
Oh Oh, Oh Oh, Oh Oh, Oh Oh…

That's what you want– a church girl who can fill up
jeans like Reesy Cup fill candy wrappers
& if she smell like Christmas too

Dog, you better than safe. But if she
breakin mirrors like Shrek
& you still want to hit it

in that case, yeah
you might wanna
strap up.

Twenty4/7

(Semi-ChocolateCity)

Friday, August 6, 2004
14th & U Streets, NW
12:35 A.M.

Mohammed & Sidi on the grill
Billy & Basie on the box.

Two brothers run by.
One chases the other–

falls so hard outside, it shakes
the restaurant's insides.

A nine in his hand hits the ground
like a wrench without the ting.

He gets up, makes a fumble recovery
runs even faster.

"Did you see that?" Two stunned
white people ask me.

I'm not sure if they mean the chase
or the fall–

or what they want me to do about it.
I hear one of them, on a cell say

"we're so lost, we're in the Ghe…"
& then she buries her voice

so as not to offend me. Voyeurs–
I think to myself.

Where are the gentrification police
when you need them?

Party of Black

Dear Hussy, Heifer, Ho, Sister Sambo, waitress who got upset, after my party of black self statued into tile, waiting for service at your restaurant. I am not grudge bearing (as in wishing hemorrhoids on your bucket headed children). I cannot be sure you even have children. Although, I am sure, if you did they would be bucket headed. I am not writing you this letter to air your septic-scented dirty wash in public. That would be unchristian. See, I went to the midweek service and the Pastor clearly spoke on longsuffering. So, I'm not going to mention how even roaches wash their hands after eating at your spot. I won't be broadcasting the address of your bile breathed establishment– the Diner located at 2453 18th Street NW, Washington, DC 20009. I won't even hint at how your bouncer boyfriend (probably an inbred cousin) threatened to dribble me for simply trying to get your attention, and how if he had touched me, I would have put my foot so far up his Barney Fife ass he would have been coughing up shoe polish.

No, I have laid those burdens down.

Harriet Tubman's Email 2 Master

>Subject: directions to the new place

go
down past glass
ground in your salt shaker

make a right
between
arsenic sweet tea swallows

i am easy to find.
just take the fork where

mothers kill their babies
to keep them safe from you

and
look for
windows growing shotguns.

Papa's Got A Brand New Pen

Speak truth on the good foot– say it loud
children
of
wooden
bellies,
children
of
Cinque's
sword.
Children
speak truth on the good foot– say it loud.

Memo 4 GOP Preachers

If homosexuality is wrong
then stealing elections is wrong.

If homosexuality is wrong
then killing Iraqi children is wrong.

If homosexuality is wrong
then half of your choir directors are wrong

& dodging your sermons
is right.

Yogi Speaks From Occupied Jellystone

Mr. Ranger, I was here with Boo Boo
before you came with fences.

No aiming arms will keep your
pic-a-nic baskets safe

because the park
belongs to me.

What SueKeithia Wrote in Social Studies

(WhenTupacDidnotDie)

My sixth grade report is on Mr. Hugo Chavez and Mr. Tupac Shakur since you said we had to write about something happening in New Jersey. The newsman said that Mr. Hugo wants to give poor folks some oil and Mr. Tupac is going to help him out by putting him in one of his raps. The man said that the President is mad about it too and calling them names and stuff. I don't understand why everybody fighting. If Mr. Hugo wanted to give me some oil, I would say thank you. A lot of times my mother asks me to put some oil in my hair and we don't have any. That gets on my nerves cause it's not even my fault we run out. My sister with her big head self always be taking more than she need and it's not just me who says she has a big head. Leroy on the 9th floor says she has a big head. Nikki on the 12th floor says she has a big head. Jada on the 20th says she has a big head. She say my sister have a big mouth too, but I know it ain't no bigger than hers cause when she saw me kiss Leroy in the hallway that time she went and told everybody at school, everybody in the building, everybody in Newark seem like, in just one night. She made me so mad I started to pop her in her big mouth, but I didn't cause she really my friend and most the time she be looking out for me when I'm on the playground. You need friends on the playground. I think Mr. Tupac knows that. He has a nice smile. I think if he was my friend nothing bad would ever happen to me. Anyway, I don't know if the President right to be so mad over some hair grease. Even if it's good hair grease. But if you ask me, if somebody act like they want to give you something, and you need it, you should try not to be too mean to them.

Even Revolutionaries Need Pillows

(MedinaDreams)

you coco piña satin over dimpled comforter hips
pillowcase of Africa in my hands

you goose down of bottomless pink
where I plant my dreams like seeds

are the reason revolutionaries
need their sleep.

Confessions

(4C)

When you're away

my hand is
free throw steady

my voice is
New York chill & dew

my back is
goal post straight

my chest is
concretized & steel

but when I
sleep, it's always on

your side of the bed.

A Time to Kiss

(afterKingSolomon)

Under
the sun
I
scuffed my
spirit, ran
my soul
over chasing
after the
wind– a
camera blink
of fame,
a thimble
sip of
power. And
how much
happiness
was measured?
And what
was good
that came
of it?
Until your
lips, nothing.
At least
nothing I
recall, after
guava jelly
kisses and
mending
under
the sun.

The Ice Cream Man

(4C)

Hot fudge
falls over

sweet staccato breath

whipped cream whistles
stutters,
          drips.

Oh how I love the taste
of cherries in the evening.

The Celestial Pound
(WhatDerrick,Fred&AlanSaidAboutTheSisters)

for stop signs in their hips
lips like cinnamon bread

for magnets in their walk
our eyes   held hostage

for lambs wool petals
on Moses Women stems

we lift our fists, bow our
heads and offer up

a pound
to heaven.

Love & Basketball

(4Cliff)

Maybe it's the bounce bounce boom, backboard bang
or sweet sweaty grit ground in hard hard wood.
We stop and go, stop and go, jook, jump, hang
like baseline was the rock where Moses stood.
Maybe it's the pill, a world in our palms
or hoop hooptie dreams of golden goose nets.
We pick & roll, pick & roll, pass, fake, calm
pull up, beat Jordan, fade away and—yes!
Game seven in the playoffs of our minds.
6 or 60, the clock is broken here.
It's a Spalding of youth where dreams own time.
When long shots fall, old is always next year.
Though legends may pass up under the ball
trash talk and rim are always ten feet tall.

Naptural

Conk my soul CJ–
lie or no lye
iron me dark & lovely.

Fry my esteem CJ.
Burn my neck 100 years long.
Madame, relax me.

I will still be tense
I will still be
fake.

I will always go back
to Africa.

Reflections: A River In Africa

(afterSteveHalle&Vie)

Being black in Africa, and HIV positive, is no longer a shocking matter. It has become as commonplace as the flu, only deadlier. Although they comprise only 10% of the world's population, Africans constitute more than 60% of the AIDS-infected population. As a result of colonialism, healthcare spending for Africans in Africa has historically been inadequate, leaving a legacy of high mortality in many regions. Much more HIV/AIDS related education is needed in Africa since no policy or law alone can combat this HIV/AIDS related discrimination. Many governments in sub-Saharan Africa denied that there was a problem for years, and are only now starting to work towards solutions. Without a unified plan of action, cemeteries will swell with the dead.

****

Being black in America, and HIV positive, is no longer a shocking matter. It has become as commonplace as the flu, only deadlier. Although they comprise only 12% of the US population, African Americans constitute more than 50% of the AIDS-infected population. As a result of racism, healthcare spending for Africans in America has historically been inadequate, leaving a legacy of high mortality in many regions. Much more HIV/AIDS related education is needed in America since no policy or law alone can combat this HIV/AIDS related discrimination. Many politicians in the United States government denied that there was a problem for years, and are only now starting to work towards solutions. Without a unified plan of action, cemeteries will swell with the dead.

Dwarfophobic

Snow White and the seven dwarfs are hiding
something. Not that I'm one to spread rumors
but Chile, everybody in the woods
ought to know, there's more going on in that
house than singing. Yeah girl, Prince Charming came
late to the party. Well no, I cain't say
I actually saw anything – cept
Grumpy taking out the trash – but it was
how he took it out, see? One night, I had
to call the police on em – I surely did.
They was a dancing with each other, all
smiley in they front yard. It was just sick.
No, they didn't arrest them, but you cain't
tell me Sleepy gets that tired from cooking.

What Branches Know

(4Melanie)

Branches know wings get
weary; hold their arms up for
butterflies landing.

Mississippi Fretless

Neck smooth
as rosewood
earrings black,

tuning my hands
turning my hands
tremble at the

tension, round
midnight, earlobes
and Mississippi delta.

I am eyes closed
in her rhythm
changes, and I

have to get the
moves right
and it has to be fretless.

Her voice is
made for
moonlight.

Her dress is
nothing but
a glaze.

Help me Jaco
Help me Jesus
hold her as I should–

improvise, resonate
swing, til every note
speaks heartbeats

my hands
become
her strings.

Monica

I breathe her
wet & silver
saint & lover

as seagulls kite
on invisible strings
catching fries.

Somewhere
D'Angelo asks
How does it feel?

It feels neon
eternal, pacific
as rod leans pier.

It feels mourners
bench, this platform–
healing

wading on wooden
legs, over call
and response waves.

Under moon, over sea
candy cane streetlights
watch rails for kisses.

They are never disappointed.

Where carousel horses
dance for hallelujah arms
of children

I am never disappointed.

Below the ocean road
Monica reminds me.
I am one of them.

Puzzle

This puzzle
boxed without
the rib shaped piece
falls in your kiss, complete.

Unsinkable

(4Randall&MMS)

After visiting Mbembe in his page ward
Ran says, *They'll probably remember us
when we're dead,* and we laugh–

poets– laughing like the Titanic band
when asked why they played on.

Along This Branch

(4Avon&Wendy)

Along this branch, we are born to bud
bounce moonlight from our fingers.

Along this branch, this wild electric branch
we are born to seek– soak symphonies of sun
only for a season.

But even when we fall, the earth remembers
how magnificent we were.

about Jessica Horn

Jessica Horn is a poet and feminist advocate with roots in Uganda's Mountains of the Moon and the shadows of New York's Yankee stadium.She works in Africa and internationally on initiatives advancing sexual rights, ending violence against women, supporting women living with HIV and ensuring women's rights in peacebuilding. Jessica has performed and published her work in activist and artistic platforms in the African region, Europe as well as the USA and her prose-poem, "Dreamings," was profiled in the International Museum of Women's online exhibition Imagining Ourselves. She won the Sojourner Poetry Prize, judged by June Jordan in 2001, for her poem "Dis UN: For Rwanda" and, in 2009 the IRN Fanny Ann Eddy Poetry Prize for her poem "They have killed Sizakele."

author statement

Speaking in Tongues was my first published collection and, I have to say, perhaps like most writers, I was worried about whether my words were 'worthy' of print! Given my hesitations it was a relief to work with Nii who lent an expert editorial eye, helping tighten the language and deal with the perennial challenge of line breaks! Once in print I felt like I was armed with a gift and have taken the collection with me on my many travels as an activist, reading from it and distributing it to people who welcome more African women's voices in print.

kudos
winner of
Sojourner Poetry Prize (2001)
IRN Fanny Ann Eddy Poetry Prize (2009)

Speaking in Tongues

Jessica Horn

First Published: 2007
Series Number: 06
Editor: Nii Ayikwei Parkes

Speaking in Tongues

And I touched her hand, like a forked stick
On water lilies on the lake of Ntuntu
Which automatically draw towards you as you pull a little.

Namukwata hamukono nk'endeesi,
Nk'akafunjo k'omunyanja ya Ntuntu,
Aka basika kunu nikeereeta.

excerpt from *Whose Love Answers Mine*
– Timothy Bazarrabusa

one: epidermis

"O my body, make of me always a [wo]man who asks questions!"
– Frantz Fanon, *Black Skin, White Masks*

(be)longing

"My home travels with the people I own, who offer me heaven"
– Pumla Dineo Gqola

It began with mountains. A landscape that offered itself on and on in the ambers and golds of dry wheat and drought. Donkeys lumbering at the bottom of desiccated valleys, making pathways of dust. Mountains and maize.

(my memory begins in mountains......)

She dreamt of rain. Drops falling at the end of rainy season when the termites would fly out and dance.

It began with the moon. Mountains. Red earth and banana trees. Women with bent backs clearing the ground for the coming harvest, the smell of scented butter rubbed lightly into their skin after the morning bath.

She dreamt of bougainvilleas. Aching fuchsia petals wrapping themselves around the fences of church yards. An elderly gardener pruning vines with his chapped hands.

It began with a ray of sun hitting faded letters on a main road which read: 'Welcome to the Equator'. Equator. The middle point. *Milieu.* My home.

I begin in the middle,
unravel into the kaleidoscope of the many *we*s

Epidermal offerings

Sometimes I feel
you have
stolen
my breath

an asthmatic evening
and I am left to my limbs
a toenail, knuckle
wedged beneath
the stitches of my
yellow cotton blouse
neighbouring skin cells
I don't know as
my own.

If I could breathe
I could chart the smell of bonded labour
know its geography
Bangkok to Port-au-Prince
the outskirts of Paris

can I call you (the
fingers that mourn
for their remembrance)
how can I name you (my
coincidental kin)?

sometimes I feel
you have stolen
my breath

caught me on the
inhalation,
transposed my air
onto daytime street
corners in Manila
where I watch
juvenile elders
offer their six-year-old-thighs
watch business men accepting, in
opium anaesthesia
precipitated down to bile
and bleeding,
syllables fail me.

if I could breathe
I could name you
if I could breathe
I could name you

trembling hazardously
I gasp
the lifesongs
of
dislocated digits
    limbs in the exile of a forgotten caress
sometimes I feel
my breath rushing back.
in the vapour of these mornings
I can hold you,
hum petals
along the contours
of
aching skin

Salt

(for Oul, Elian, Amadou)

Birth brings blues
in the scarlet canals of its passage
bruises and blisters call in the night

She came over pacific oceans
Cambodia to LA
clothing tight around her
refugee limbs
with every newborn tug
she feels at her breast
nausea rises
red
appears on the walls
red-rouge-Khmer-crying

bruises and blisters call in the night

He came
through gulf streams
reciting prayers to the exiled saints
of Cuban cathedrals
his young fingers
clinging to an innertube
batista chants wrap around him like seaweed
salt-sand-CNN
stick to his conquistador skin

birth brings blues
in the scarlet canals of its passage
bruises and blisters call in the night

Another returns
over Atlantic oceans
soaked in the silent sirens of New York's assassins
19 holes through his
charcoal body
flesh embraces bullets
in the wails of
Guineé's coast

bullets salt rocks flesh
salt sand seaweed skin

these are the fossilised fables
that wash up on the shores of the north
immigrant dreams of
home and safety
blasted from their saline sanctuaries
onto sidewalks
patrolled
by shadows

Oul, Elian, Amadou
scrape out a place
in these hostile ports,
drift blistered and bruised
through the scarlet canals of birth's passage
calling out blues
to the northern night

dis U.N (for Rwanda)

we could call it
the shattering of limbs at 4 p.m.
　　　exorcism after a long day at church
it would sit uneasily
in our stomachs
but we could forget
as we sat down
for the evening meal.

　'cleansing'
had a smoother sound
like a laying on of hands
a righteous burial.

we could call it many things
and we did

revelling in lyrical mastery and
the art
of
　side
　　step

six
seven
eight hundred thousand voices
hum into the red clay of the hillsides

a word

six
seven
eight hundred thousand voices

hum into the red clay of the hillsides
a word

that sutures meaning to their deaths
a word only they are willing to utter
a word
a word

genocide

haiku

if Elian was
Haitian bullets would have met
him on cold sand beach

sista, why do you run?
(dedicated to those women who have not survived sexual violence)

been a long time
in these bruised bones
long time in my rituals
of burnt eyes
and painted smile.

been a long time, sista
shivering in bathtubs
pleading
breathe, child, breathe
pleading
bathwater cleanse
bathwater cleanse
pleading
breathe, child, breathe

been a long time
hanging onto
the echo
of heartbeat
searching for safety
in the laughter of women.

man still come
you know.
day-time phone call
scorpion sting
mosquito bite
at midnight
sometimes

see the wound
swelling
across my aching breasts
my soft thighs
turned rough
with time
and
nightmares.

been a long time
in these bruised bones, sista.
look at me
as I fade from my own eyes.

just another woman
searching for the
light.

haiku

(crimson)

he paints red over
her mouth completes the canvas
of death-by-silence

lament in ebony

arms are meant for embracing
minds to cultivate dreams of flight

I see you blackchild
ebony skin and white teeth
resident of shadowlands
the carcass of Gulu town

morning has mothered no millet,
afternoon no tea
howling belly full of gunfire
rumbling like raging sky

arms are meant for embracing
minds to cultivate dreams of flight

I see you blackchild
camouflage and swagger
patrolling Harlesden pavements
        playground of rebels with no cause

dawn rises on broken bottles
dusk on spliffs and rock
howling belly full of gunfire
yearning for a new high

lady's tired of singing the blues

(for Miles, James, Tyson)

muse
muse
music-man
be-bopper
chart-stopper
tip-top of the
tales she used to tell
  just a little scratch
alarm? un-needed. He's taking care of me
ever feel your trumpet wail as deep
her kind-of-blues?

king
king
king
of the ring
around her finger,
hear it cost her more than gold.
I know why
the caged bird can't sing
boxer got it beat an indigo hue

yeah, you feel good
knowing I wouldn't
yeah, you feel nice
knowing I couldn't

Well.

Man
I feel like screaming, hell I feel like crying.
I've been mistreated[1]
but I am sick to death of dying!
Man I feel like leaving,
man watch me flying
'Cos I'm giving up tarnished mornings
and the sound of my voice lying

Man I plan on leaving
man watch me flying
'Cos I'm well past paying my dues
and lady's tired of singing the blues.

[1](Adapted from Bessie Smith's 'Moonshine Blues')

two: pores

"Soy un monton de cosas santas, mesclada con cosas humanas"
"I am a mountain of saintly things, mixed with pieces of the mundane"
- Mercedes Sosa, Yo soy

willow-limbed women
descendants of grace
and equatorial sunshine

arms spread wide
   in the ecstasy of early-evening dance
arms arched upwards
   like the horns of Ankole cattle

women of soured milk
and planting song
keepers of the mountain
fire

Uganda haikus (sunrise to 9 p.m.)

I
sunrise. red earth crows
as loud as the rooster for
raindrops, falling seeds

II
day awakens her
fresh limbs, lays out promises
of millet and tea

III
Bakongo women
glide to market backs taut as
ndingidi strings

IV
schoolmaster passes
students tremble single file
small eyes starched silent

V
women's gossip swells
essential as *matoke*
in the midday heat

VI
needle drowning in
kanzu cloth, as delicate
as the call to prayer

VII
moonrise. ageing man
pacing towards home weary
as the day's gunfire

Good noses

How they admired delicate curves
shunned nostrils that flared
out like the buttocks
of cows

sang praises
to sleek bridges
stretching from their crescent
moon hairlines like Ruwenzori
peaks in spring

as childhood taunts fermented
in harvest heat,
as rage shook the steel of *pangas*
like millet in October storms

Prayer

(meditations on HIV/AIDS in Uganda I)

Prayer
is what she is now
melodic promises from an imported cassette
dactari yesu dactari
mganga yesu mganga
anaponya yesu anapnoya
the kiswahili is
   as familiar to her tongue
as glucose powder
   and the warmth of fresh milk

Jesus my doctor, Jesus my healer, Jesus

breathing has become her sustenance
inhalations from Psalms
     and a verse from Job that reads

have pity on me, have pity on me
o you my friends, for the hand of
God has touched me

prayer

is all she is now
unable to suture skin
to the rhythmic murmurs of
dying

in silence
at midday
she repeats

daughter, your faith has made you well
go in peace.

Dreamings
(meditations on HIV/AIDS in Uganda II)

I
In the dream of a dream. Somewhere inside the coarse melody of
breathing, there is a woman. In a dream of a dream, somewhere, there is
a woman weeping. The cotton of her *busuti* is creased at the knees after
hours of kneeling by the bedside. She is holding tea in one hand, and in
the dusk she drinks it. A kerosene lamp lights the motion of hand to cup
to sighing lips.

II
In a dream of a dream. Somewhere.

III
Three men lean against the bar, focused on the cool froth of their
afternoon drinks. Kenyan beer, Tusker. Their suits are freshly pressed and
their talk is pungent like the smell of overripe mangoes. Ageing roosters,
they speak about the news of the past weeks, and between the gossiping
they mourn. Grace's daughter is sick and she has gone home to the village
in Ankole. The rains are heavy and the men hope that the bus will reach
the village by nightfall. The road must have been churned to mud by now.

IV
An old woman murmurs short prayers as she watches her daughters
pounding groundnuts. It is nearing five o'clock and she wears a dress
of ochre and green that seems at peace with the red clay of the hillsides.
Her son Joseph will be marrying on Sunday and the community will
be expecting a grand feast. The millet has been ground and is ready to
cook but ten kilos of *matoke* still need to be cut and prepared by the day.
Her oldest daughter pauses, turns to look at her and she remembers her
husband who passed only last year. She grows weary remembering the
hours of cooking, washing, digging she did to support her family — yet
her husband still sought satisfaction outside of the house. Her prayers
resume with the pounding.

V

In a dream of a dream. Somewhere between heartbeat and the coarse melody of breathing, there is a woman. In a dream of a dream, somewhere, there is a woman telling stories. The days grow long in each syllable she offers. Sometimes she speaks bullets that recall the days of armies that swarmed the country like locusts, destroying what they could. Other times she speaks Nile waters that brought *wazungu* so far from their homes. They say she can speak injections and pills that bring the fever down, and bring life back for another day. Today she is speaking in reams of colourful cotton. Bodies are being cleansed for burial and she will clothe them in the hues of mountain flowers.

VI

In a dream of a dream, somewhere. There is a woman.

three: pulse

"Freedom: A way of being, a voice, a body to behold"
                    - Yvonne Vera, *The Stone Virgins*

You are warm rain and harvest melody
I am cool clay and ocean breeze

drops

fall

into

open

vessel

You are red mud: I am moist earth
You are warm breeze: I am clear voice

Haiku

(amber)

Constantly birthing
blooming butterflies from your
hands of raging fire

let me

birth flame trees
on your
fingers

breathe nectar
in crevices of wild

honey

3 simple tools:
    palate, hand, canvas of the body

3 gifts given:
    pigment, touch, healing wind

3 times born:
    painter, lover, *mganga* of my flesh

Night blooms

Forests grow
on the inside
of my urban skin.
Moon begs
for its immortal light

and I
succumb,
bathe with fireflies

in the rhapsody
of an indigo sky.

I have tamed
steel and tungsten
tempted echoes
in the ebony caverns of the city

Tonight,
I have conquered dew and darkness
I am molten, ready for your lava touch.

Ye ye o

(between a dancer and a drummer)

yellow petal falls
into oshun's river,
flows golden

*

waterspirit awakens inside
our pores bloom with drumbeats
melodious skin

*

I cover my hair with
white cloth, bathe in amber water-
falls of drumspeaksound

*

intoxicated
by space and sighs
we travel
from neck to ankle
charting
our incompleteness
our
divine humanity

*

we dreamed
we dreamed
we dreamed
we could
make love
 to music

ride high
on the sound
that   slips   off
leather and
    mango wood
old
in its sap and
skin

*

purpleblueblackpurpleblueblackbeads
purple blue black
purple blue black beads
skins beads sweat beads skin
salt wet salt skin salt wet salt
tongue. teeth. thighs.

about Denise Saul

Denise Saul was born in London. She is a poet and fiction writer. Her debut publication, White Narcissi, was Poetry Book Society Pamphlet Choice for Autumn 2007. Denise was selected for The Complete Works, a two-year mentoring and development programme for ten advanced Black and Asian poets in the UK. Her mentor was John Stammers. Denise's House of Blue (published by Rack Press) was Poetry Book Society Pamphlet Recommendation for Summer 2012. She is the winner of the 2011 Geoffrey Dearmer Prize for her poem 'Leaving Abyssinia'.

author statement

My initial meeting with Nii, the editor allowed me to think again about the subject matter of this pamphlet. Initially, I chose around twenty poems but as the editing sessions progressed, I found that only eighteen of those poems 'spoke' to each other in the collection. Nii was happy for all twenty poems to be part of the pamphlet, however I realised that a few of the poems had stopped speaking to each other. For me, editing work is not just about what can be omitted but also what can be added to a collection. The trickiest part was creating a design for the front cover. Inua and I agreed on the symbols of the seashell and pomegranate. *White Narcissi* was my first published collection of poems and the first stage of finding my voice as a poet.

kudos
winner of
Poetry Book Society Pamphlet Choice (2007)
Geoffrey Dearmer Prize (2011)
Poetry Book Society Pamphlet Recommendation (2012)

White Narcissi

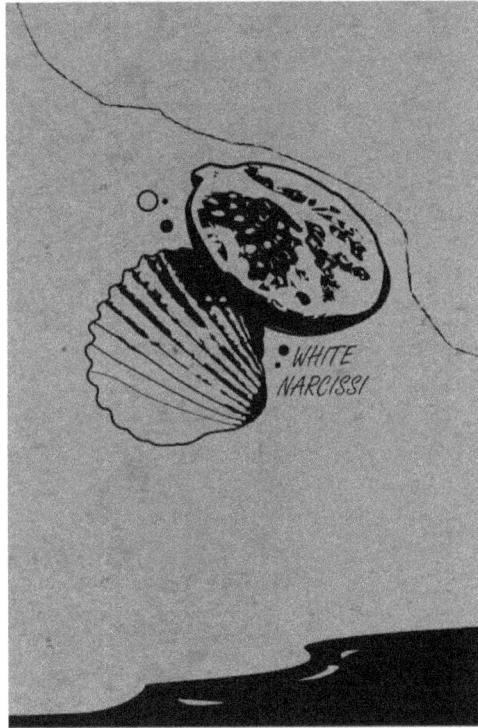

WHITE
NARCISSI

Denise Saul

First Published: 2007
Series Number: 07
Editor: Nii Ayikwei Parkes

We returned to our places, these Kingdoms,
But no longer at ease here, in the old dispensation,
With an alien people clutching their gods.

– T.S. Eliot, *Journey of the Magi.*

White Narcissi

Insects

I ask my niece why she messed up
our kitchen wall with green doodle.
She points to a squashed
bottle of washing-up liquid
in the pedestal bin.

I had turned over the next page
of Baudelaire's *Les Fleurs du Mal*
when I realised our house was too quiet
for a six-year-old playing downstairs.
Now I am asking her why.

That summer, I watched ants
stumble across the threshold of our house.
In straight military lines,
they carried grains of demerara sugar
to a colony in the garden.

Gran stopped these angry insects
from marching into our home.
She squirted detergent on the outside step.
In the afternoon, black bodies lay
like full stops on the ground.

Now I am asking my niece why
in the middle of the kitchen.
I hate flies, she shouts.
I wanted to drown them.
I strike her cheek.

Now I know how those fragile bodies felt
as they fell into that sticky fluid.
Delicate dipterans flapped
until torn thoraces stuck to green liquid.
My niece asks me why but I can't answer.

Scent of Sex

My summer dress hangs inside a wardrobe.
Its satin folds swell with the shape of me.
I rub my fingers on the shiny nub
of a button carved from mother-of-pearl.
The collar smells of cedarwood moth-balls.

We are both ten. My cousin from Kansas
wears the same ivory dress. Our starched bows
stick out behind us as small angel wings.
After art-class, we run home on damp grass.
Dandelion seeds stick to our sandals.

My best friend climbs the old rowan tree.
She tucks her gingham pinafore inside
her pants as confetti of deep russet
and burgundy leaves fall on her shoulders.
Her plaited hair smells of crushed berries.

Years on, my oldest cousin wears white.
Her bridal gown unfolds on the aisle as
a lily heavy with scent of its sex.
As I hold her veil, pollen stains my hand.

Broken Zip

Now I stand over you to smooth
the sleeves of the cardigan
you have shrunken into over the years.

With my palms, I iron out
the creased rows of purl and plain,
before closing the cardigan's zip.

Beneath the stratum of wool,
your skin feels like the delicate leaves
that cling to the fruit of a physalis.

In another season,
you dressed me. You zipped up my cardigan
as I got ready for school.

Each time, you tried to pull up the zip,
it jammed where the closure buckled
and then you pulled it down to start again.

This is what always happened:
the zip broke to reveal
a row of teeth.

When We Sleep

At night, I can hear her voice
filling our bedroom.

A laughter that starts in the belly
as she throws back her head.

Her twisted locks are black
snakes that writhe around her neck.

Sometimes, when you look at me,
I can still hear this *ha, ha, ha*.

I long to cut off her head
while she sleeps with you

and then hold it up to your face
to petrify you with her gaze.

Bodies

Once a week, somewhere along the 213 miles
of the Thames, a dead body is washed ashore.
The Guardian 15.12.04

The body of a woman floats.
She has freed herself from
the tangled weeds beneath
a small jetty in the U-bend.

A man who stood on
the bridge to look closer,
now lies next to beer cans
and crumpled carrier bags.

Putrefied, bloated flesh
rises to the surface.
Skin decays into a patina
of unfurling algae.

Maybe, tomorrow another
person will swim along.
And again, they will dredge to find
a body, a torso or a name.

Fall

You stood on the peak of my breasts
wearing wings made of paper and wax.

With arms stretched out towards
the orange dot in the sky,

you tried to fly away from me
when we talked about serious things.

Now, after the fall, I see you still flapping
scorched plumage as you battle

against heat and wind until
no feathers remain to catch the air.

Looking at Mars Through a Telescope

Can they hear my heart
as it thuds like a stone thrown
into a stream before it sinks
to the bottom and waits.

White Narcissi

Yet again, we wake from the same dream.
You are staring at yourself in a lake
surrounded by white narcissi

while I look back at you
as a reflection in Stygian waters.
All you can see are the parts of your face

as they separate from each other.
First, the eyes move apart, right
from left, ears following

each other across the lake
like pollen expelled from a swollen bud.
Next, the mouth splits into

a muffled scream that repeats around us
as we hold onto each other, shaking
as our bones turn into rocks.

Half-light

I bring a gold coin to find you.
I stand by the river's edge,
wait for the man who rows a boat
against this shoreline, black as obsidian.

I press an obolus deep into his palm;
we will not speak on this journey.
I will look for your face inside his
as we cross to the other side.

I listen to the silence,
search for your laughter in its stillness.
I will not look back into the eye of the sun
sinking into the socket of these hills.

I Must Tell You

that all my hopes from those days are
bees battering windows.

Wings squashed against the leaden pane;
their smeared bodies

hang like semi-colons
between sentences.

First Rip

I gather the first pair of tights over
the sole of my left foot, gently pulling away
creases until the gossamer fits my thighs.

Then I catch a glimpse of the first rip
on bare flesh, spilling rungs of its ladder
from toe to ankle, then from knee to thigh.

The ladder begins at the seamed toe,
and moves upwards under my short skirt,
into lines of broken thread.

I brush nail varnish on the first rung
but its redness does not stop the hole
from spreading over my skin.

Leather Belt

I buckle this belt around my waist.
As I walk to the bedroom mirror, I see
the face of Lilith who looks back at me.
I listen to a voice who tells me to cover
my ears from the hissing that grows louder.
When I touch the leather skin,
each brass eyelet stares back at me.
When I open my eyes, I see myself
walking from an orchard
that smells of rotten apples.
And later when I unfasten this buckle,
I stare at my reflection as the belt falls
and then slithers back into Adam's ribs.

Walk Home

Blisters hatch
behind heel.
I take off
my sister's
scarlet shoes
and walk home.

Lazarus

Imagine how great life would be
if you never lost anything.
The dead could reclaim what is theirs.
Breaking out of rotting boxes,
they would push through damp earth
like black-trumpet mushrooms.

Imagine, you could hold your father
as someone who has never lost.
Soiled bandages would unravel
to reveal scars from cankerous sores,
while you stretch your arms
to reclaim what is yours.

Dad

I was one when you ate
those hard seeds.

Through spring, you stayed with me.
Only I could see you laughing at my toys.

Those days smelt like
pomegranates, fresh and tart.

I dreamt that you called to me from behind a church wall.
Come with me, you whispered. But I did not.

You slipped away again
when birds flew southward.

I could not remember
those smooth hands.

Each year, as sunlight fades
I wait for your return.

Bone

After Shell, 1928 by Salvador Dali

The sea lived inside me once.
Waves slipped in, out, in
like a small foot into a shoe.

Before you throw me back,
place my opening to your ear.

Listen to the darkness inside
this gaping mouth of bone.

about Malika Booker

Malika Booker is a British writer of Guyanese and Grenadian Parentage. Her poems are widely published in anthologies and journals including: *Out of Bounds, Black & Asian Poets* (Bloodaxe 2012) and *Ten New Poets* (Bloodaxe, 2010). She has represented British writing internationally, both independently and with the British Council including New Zealand, India, and Azerbaijan. She has also written for the stage and radio. Her one-woman show *Unplanned*, toured the UK in 2007 and she was inaugural Poet in Residence at the Royal Shakespeare Company. Her collection *Pepperseed* is forthcoming from Peepal Tree Press in 2013.

author statement

Working with Nii Parkes as my pamphlet editor was aided by the fact that he is a writer with a vast experience of writing and editing his own work and he brings this to the table. His attention to detail, his labour in the service of a poem, and the fact that, in sitting together negotiating changes, I could feel my work improving was impressive. Sometimes a simple word change, shifting a comma, or repositioning a verse yielded some amazing insights. I felt that Nii's experience and instinct, as well as sensitivity to my motivations as a writer, created a pamphlet that I am extremely proud of. I had no clue about ordering of the poems and Nii's guidance created a book that I am often told can be read effortlessly from front cover to back, each poem building a rich linear narrative.

kudos

commended by
Poetry Book Society (2008)
selected as
Poet-in-Residence, Hampton Court Palace (2004)
Poet-in-Residence, Royal Shakespeare Company (2011)

Breadfruit

Malika Booker

First Published: 2007
Series Number: 08
Editor: Nii Ayikwei Parkes

Breadfruit

Letting go

They gave away the cat when I was born
took her one day in 1970 and left her.
She came back twice they say.

They loved that cat, it was hard,
yet no one remembers her name,
what she looked like, just

a blanket she carried everywhere.
There was an electric fire, my aunt said, *where
she would curl, the blanket clenched between her teeth;*

my grandmother said *cats steal babies'
breaths.* Mum saw babies mangled
by jealous cats in the hospital

where she worked, so she began
to have dreams of the cat scratching
and prodding her baby, the blanket

covered with blood. By the seventh dream,
a week before I was born,
the cat had to go, *we loved you so much*

that the cat had to go, Mum tells me
as we make the bed. A part of me feels
special, the other sorry for the cat.

I tell her she was cruel, how could you
let go of something you love?
It was practice, she says, *everyday*

you and your brothers grow older
and I'll have to let go of you.
She shakes the bedspread into the air

smoothes it with a flat palm, sits down
and starts to cry.
I remember us telling her only yesterday

to leave us to live our own lives;
I think
I know what she is talking about.

For Clara

You are Victorian Myth;
stories circle your village of exploits,
how you beat three boys at once
throwing sand in their eyes,

the time you climbed two chairs
to take food Grandma placed beyond reach,
and fell to the hard floor still chewing fast fast
to avoid detection, nursing a broken hand.

The 1959 voyage to London; Dad saw
twenty-two inch waist, buxom hips,
olive eyes; there was love and marriage
love and patients, love and parties.

Now I watch you for signs of the old
you. I sit at family
gatherings as elders send children back and forth
to fetch and carry, aunties watch pots

of chicken and salt fish smells
fill the house, long sermons bless
the food with grace and grumbles.
I sit outside circles of old uncles,

with children's high-pitched screams
as background sounds, listening
to patriarchs rumbling wisdom
drunk on rum,

look at their gold-toothed smiles
while wedding bands wave in dramatic talk
to receive sprigs of truth about the girl
you once were before me

before marriage
before
mother
you were Clara.

Me: I love the one I know
I can read her like Braille
as I am her seed dropped
watered and bloomed.

I ask you about her and through your
silence, mouth locked shut, I create
you: seeing a young woman, signs of
age thickening her waist, walking

the streets of dreary London
eyes blinking fat lines of tears
hands doubled over her stomach
moaning for God's help with her rent.

She wraps in thicker layers
binding her heart as yet another lover leaves
then sits alone under winter skies
screaming at the world, the house

noise for company in a red carpeted room
Wait   this is not about you but my quest;
a woman grappling with the hourglass
of age counting my time

to motherhood, questioning your journey
as we sit today, not as mother
and daughter; our roles
have left us; we sit as two women.

Portrait

I.
Caribbean intellectual, push-in slippers dark as the wooden floors you lacquered. Khaki long trousers, and white short sleeve shirt jack, with long strides, slow gait, *why hurry,* you always said, *life waits for you.* Short kinky afro, side parted. Dreams for houses formed furrows between your brows. Your nightly absences meant forgotten cinema trips, children and wife left waiting. Five am door taps, hushed footsteps betrayed by the crack and snap of floorboards.

II.
Foreign father, sneakers, jeans, and short sleeve shirt, first two buttons open. Hair red brown with grey tints, face lined with years, soft folds of skin loose at the throat. You are sunken, fragile. The furrows in your brow are permanent. You live alone; plan to make it big. Where are the women now, who squandered your dreams? Wife and children, long gone, across the seas, your sons walking; long strides, with slow gait, their legacy. *Why hurry?*

Sour Milk

On petrol and sour milk he ruled Guyana;
people lined up for hours outside Shell stations,
milk was banned – people waited till it was sour,
wishing, dreaming of *Tennis Rolls* and *swank.*

Nuff people gaffed, sitting on gas
cylinders in the sun, my brother and I
grumbled to an old man; how we lined up for petrol
missed playing cricket and hopscotch in the pasture.

He said, You think this is hard, girle?
You didn't see de country blaze in de sixties
niggers was burning coolie house, I barely get out
holding a cutlass and mi daddy's shoe.
How this country can burp evil, yes.
Look at Jim Jones, all them people, dead ah bush;
told us, Knowledge flies and frees prisoners;
told us, President Burnham wants the country feed she self,
he making a better place for we children play hopscotch.

One day Daddy came home with sardines, milk
juicy fruit; banned food from Burnham's house.
Our innocence burst. The revolution was a lie.

My Father's Letter

I picture you writing, eyes stained,
glazed with untreated cataract, writing
during power cuts by kerosene lamps
or candles. Scraping your life between
the faint blue lines of faded yellow paper.

Mum said my brothers got their letter,
but being boys they will not respond
until it is too late. They will speak
to gravestones of regrets.

I got the letter - nine folded A4
pages blaming yourself for slammed doors
and bad choices. Telling stories of your dad
playing silly games, shouting up drain pipes
Who's down there? and you would shout

Who's up there asking who's down here?
which you now know
were your dad's shy attempts
to create tender moments.

I don't remember those mistakes.
I recall riding your shoulders,
your night stories, I spent years
as a little tomboy
modelled on you.

Lately I have become cold.
Could be the winter or damp
in the room, your letters put off
till tomorrow, and a year later

I watch the paper and pen
adding the letter to yet another thing
to do.

Garden Poems

Hampton Court Palace, September 2004

The Carving: honeysuckle twilight parties

"No wood was finer than yew for magic wands..."
– Margaret Baker, 'The Folklore of Plants'

A head, carved into the Yew's trunk, intricate
like art sculpted by God. Head bowed in prayer,
its features solemn, one hand propping a chin,
lying on brown pillows.

At night I imagine you awaken,
call fairy friends to your lawn of dreams.
Dusk is your time, wood nymph, child of the fairies.

At twilight, you plunge into the pond,
to chortle under the fountain.
You grab the nearest fairy by her waist,
then waltz among the dewdrops.
Dancing to sweet duets
between wind and leaves.

I know your delightful chuckles, you guffaw
at the owl's hoot. The garden is yours,
magic sizzles the air. When night marries

day your lament will begin. You will curl back
blubbering. Curve into the trunk, a ghostly sculpture,
a shadow of yourself, your face mournful,
frozen, weary, hidden till dusk.

The Maze: Absurd Charade

It starts out fun,   then
there is the same dead
end.   The same two women
again.   Walk
another way. Pass
the same women. Meet
the same dead end.   Smile,
like you know the way
out.   Turn a corner
another dead   end,
turn back,   it's
the same two women.
Now you feel like
a wasp, hitting itself
over and over
against a glass pane,   knowing
there is a way out
of this maze,
desperate   to find
it. So you pass
the same women   again,
smile   vaguely,
not fooling anyone.

The Maze: Maze etiquette

Black iron fence, coated with leaves, a manicured hedge patterned in square blocks, bordering pathways. Peering through the green mesh, to glimpse people moving, see a concrete bench - the maze centre. See the exit sign, right there through the gap but can't get to it. By now the mind plays tricks, I have passed here before. People's words carry though the maze as if next to me, but I am alone on my path. *Let's go left, then right; mummy I wanna go this way; exit, see I am right.* I hear splatters of Chinese, Italian, German, and Dutch. Imagine they are saying the same things. Nothing here is simple.

The Maze: Angel of the labyrinth

I am still,
lost in this labyrinth,
when he arrives, eyes dancing
mischief, impish smile,
his wings a Jan Sport rucksack,
halo a Nike cap,
his robe an oversized Lakers
t-shirt with khaki combat shorts.
He is easily seven years old.
He stops
in front of me, asks
if I am lost,
tells me to follow him,
walks ahead
looking back
to see if I am
still there,
his expanding cheeks
entice me to smile back at him.
He leads me out like a lamb
leading a shepherd.
At the entrance I say thanks,
blink, and he is gone.
The gatekeeper tells me
I am not the first,
he has been saving lost souls
all afternoon.

The Magical Pathway

Where the bench lies inscribed; *"Our friend and colleague Peggy Jones,*
who worked as a gardener in these gardens from 15 May '61 - 13 Jan, '78"

1
her spirit lies mute
in this magical garden
paved with broken stones

2
a secluded grove
green leaves hang low on lovers
the sun filters in

3
bamboo hideaway
cradles lovers on benches
she sits looks ponders

4
her tribute brings tears
lingers in this silent cove
honeysuckle scent

5
the leaves golden brown
knock each other like shack shack
their love affair ends

The Fountain: a monument

I will sit here like we used to.
Sit, watch the waters.
Sit whilst seasons change, see
my life slipping to meet her. See
her as we used to be yesterday.
Today there is just an empty house
children grown.
She loved that fountain
the ducks, trout, blackbirds
wading and soaring
like she did when cancer
took her after fifty-two years
of marriage. I watch
the water, its tranquil lull
soothes me.

This Kiss

The kiss shakes me every time
creeps up after long intervals
A chance dance, suddenly you arrive,

Dancing partners, the safe kind,
hiding subtle attractions, guarded.
The kiss shakes me every time;

lands right, soft, plays on my mind.
Me leaning up, hips shaking, fused.
A chance dance, suddenly you arrive.

Days later, I awake to find
my pillows soaked, lonely, wistful.
The kiss shakes me every time;

to dark corners, silk, music, me
with you, vulture of hearts.
In this chance dance, suddenly, you arrive

with this snap, quick flutter of lips
shaking my single blues. I wish...
The kiss shakes me every time.
A chance dance, suddenly, you...

Clasped

I remember stepping
into your house
on my twenty fifth birthday,
you pulling me

into your kitchen from the October cold,
twisting my buttons through tight holes,
your fingers pushing and flexing,
then spinning me into the centre of the room.

I fell into you, stretched my arms
around your waist, hands marooned
in your girth, lost in the space, looking
like a child hugging an adult
not a woman her lover.

From your wrist, you unwrapped
a red bandana, covered my eyes,
saying trust me, asking if it was too tight
cupped my hands, lifted them to my waist,
palms upturned. Guess, you said.

I wondered what you had done:

The night before we'd dined
on Cheese & Onion Pringles. We had
no money for Chinese, and I told you
I craved surprises every birthday.

I remember hearing our breathing,
water dripping from the tap
onto the pile of unwashed dishes,
the drone of the fridge.

You slid something across my palm
tickling, making me giggle, my
fingers curled to feel; a chain I guessed.
You laughed, untied the bandana,

I saw a silver bracelet, expensive,
Happy Birthday, you clasped it.
I promised never to take it off,
to keep it forever.

Four or five years later, outside
Woolworths, by the automatic glass door,
a man looks me in the eye, points down
to where the bracelet lies,

clasp broken.
Shopping forgotten,
I rush home
and call you, near tears,
willing you to pick up. When
your voice answers, I gabble
about the broken bracelet,
then I pause. You are silent,

a woman's voice in the background
asks, Who is it? A wrong number, you reply.
Sorry, I say, fingers clutching the phone
I look at the clasp;

it's broken beyond repair.

Hungerford Bridge

Since you jumped
I have wondered
what death is like.

On sweltering nights, hay fever attacks;
I awake starved of wind, oxygen scarce,
listless, clogged up by a sticky cork, gasping,
gaping mouth working like a fish,
my tongue coated with white spots
where my mouth attempted to keep me alive.
And I fight, crying, trumpeting my nostrils
with mighty heaves.

Then I think of you.

For three years you have been
submerged,
missed your step off the tall red barrier,
you strode into nothing,
blinked and you were air walking,
feet scissoring, landing
like a life raft on the Thames,
pinstriped suit ballooned,

brief case dislodged.
For a moment   time stopped.
Now every time I walk across Hungerford Bridge
I see you step, land, and balloon.

I took a bath the other day
and thought of you

landing.

Vigil

Her youngest daughter searches for a funeral dress
and white veil. Her eldest daughter folds in, her
son disappears into heroin. I ask only that my aunt
wait for me the way her mother waited for her, holding
death back with laboured breath, eyes fixed ahead

living to see her daughter that last time. I ask her to
wait so I can watch her steady fingers rotate
the rosary beads, kiss the baby hair by her ear,
smile when she tells me she is scared. I don't want her
to be alone. I am confident, like god. Packing

for my early morning flight at 3am, the phone rings.
She's gone. I am calm in acceptance.

Today I walk along the river Thames,
following a procession, nostalgic as the season dies,
watching rust coloured leaves litter as Indian gods, samba
dancers, and fish lanterns glide in the night.
I walked in this sea of bodies last year,

saying poems about crossroads
to veil faced Orishas, lifeless puppets. I walked
dressed in white like her face covered in that coffin.
I walked preparing for my vigil, ticking off hours
to my flight. It's a year today.

I knew she would wait, but she slipped out
real quiet, gone she own way.

Identity

Suckled on mammy's taetae
nourished on granny's stories.
From wet moon-light kisses
on broken bent backs and all embracing laps.
Backstairs black outs, power cuts,
obliterated streetlights,
magnified sounds at night,
presented perfect setting, for storytelling
beginning crick crack,
then the story end and the wire bend

Who am I?

The story goes, sapodilla-hued,
brown-toned, woman child hair like
Caribbean aerial, tuned into BBC:
BRITISH
BIRTH COMPLEX
whilst satellite dish hugged memories of zinc roofs
where navel cord lay buried
back a yard of Granny's shack
protected by rain, wind spears and violent clouds, beneath
Guyanese coconut trees, forced to transmit to British soil.

She knew who she was:

Molasses flowing, nutmeg-shaded, woman child.
Did her veins not flow through the Demerara River
from Buxton Freetown to Caricou where
her bloodline grew fertile, hardened
upright women who gracefully coursed through
life? Angels protected her path
like shepherds tending God's flocks.

This mental paradise of older Shango priestesses
lit candles for future generations,
creating a rich calabash of history makers.

Wire waist, little and talawa,
showing her motion left, right and centre,
her armour of net wrapping her like clinging vine,
thorns protecting petals made for sipping.
Loneliness cloaked her soul
so she poured her love on men going nowhere,
wandering souls, brothers who thought
women's life flows theirs to control.
She was widow's peaked woman child, cloaked
in royal sexiness, innocence wrestling with experience.

She was a maker of life's chocolate
dreams, crafting pictures of palm
lines and heartaches, a magician crafting
reality from illusions; she preached from
pulpits of dimly lit stages pulled
from her memory; chanted in oral ceremony.

about Janett Plummer

Janett Plummer is an accomplished performer and a multi-slam winner. She has featured at venues such as the Barbican, Tate Modern, Poetry Café and Paradiso (Amsterdam). A winner of the Gwendolyn Brooks Annual Award (2005), her work is featured in many anthologies including *Flowers on a Shoestring* and *A Storm Between Fingers* (flipped eye, 2007). Janett is the founder of Inspired Word – a women's writing collective – and she leads poetry and creative writing workshops for children and adults.

author statement

The process of editing *Lifemarks* was a series of emails furiously shuttling to and fro between myself and my editor, Niall O Sullivan. It began with a few disagreements, debates about the use of apostrophe, and I was on my way. I learnt about editors' choices as he highlighted themes and threads that persist in my writing that I wasn't consciously aware of. One stumbling block was the insertion of "Unpicked," an emotional seven-part poem that I thought altered the tone of the pamphlet. I fought, argued and petulantly stuck out my bottom lip, but Niall wanted me to be brave enough to show the raw and scary. Although I emerged with a bloodied nose, those poems are the ones that have resonated the most with people who have read my work. Niall encouraged me to look beyond the embarrassment, shame and exposure I felt when I wrote it, he insisted I put it out there as a part of my journey and for that I am grateful.

kudos
winner of
Gwendolyn Brooks Annual Open Mike Award (2005)

lifemarks

life
marks

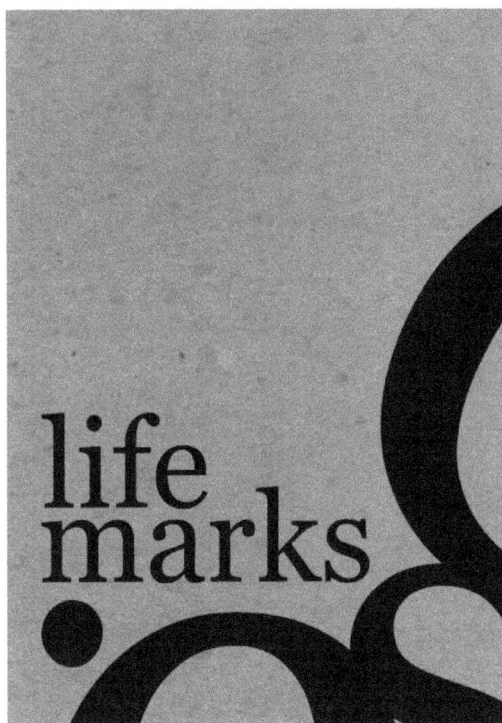

Janett Plummer

First Published: 2009
Series Number: 09
Editor: Niall O'Sullivan

lifemarks

Unpicked

Maida

Maida dirt, as red as unripe plums,
bauxite my mother couldn't wait to escape
strays into my sandals, lingers
and settles under the arch of my foot.

From a distance, footsteps shadow me;
behind the roll of my hips
my bottom sits atop my legs,
perched on the dip of my back.

Shoulders – wide and upright –
counterbalance heavy cleavage,
strides of *self surance*. Upturned
milk-bottle calves power forward.

You're Kitty's daughter, she calls.
Her words bowl me over
from their distance, in this place
of sameness, poverty and heat.

She is certain I belong
to the woman who left 43 years ago,
same shape as the one I wear well.

...and then as if by magic,
a year after you came,
the lifemarks appeared.
Two-inch long silver brown,
thick shiny lines
scored my flesh.

Mother nature has a way
of inflicting her sense of humour,
giving post-birth presents:
a flatter stomach
and smaller breasts
than I could wish for
– re-shaped.

Long baths revealed
three tiny silver lines in a row,
the smallest barely visible to the eye,
so if a future lover were to trace
his hand over my stomach,
past the glint of gold/diamond navel
ring, he would feel the raised contours,
the dip and fold of them,
the smooth yet rippled texture.

These marks are a sign
that you are here, etched
deep, engraved in my flesh,
a memento of your life
marking mine.

Imprint

Sunday morning, the smell of you lingers
long after my bath has swirled clockwise down the hole.

My lips are still pink from kissing,
muscles jump at the thought of yesterday's lust.

Aftershave pressed itself into my blouse;
slow-dancing, my cleavage traps it.

Tongue trails of saliva run towards
the pool of sweat that collects in the dip of my back.

Lazy smiles and grinning eyes
make me wish away my celibacy.

I had forgotten the day dreaming thing you do
when a new lover imprints you.

The feelings only a new lover can remind you of
cocoon me – until the weekend.

Red String

She's celebrating Jesus
- in a G-String,

hollas, whoops and hallelujahs,
as dancehall makes way for divinity.

They're singing real loud
like a favoured Mary J tune,

praying for sins
they've yet to commit.

They're bringing all they've got,
voices failing

as they sway in time,
arms flailing.

Sister Joyce eyes a too-high heel,
a skin design peeps from a chest

where they've tattooed
his word on their hearts.

Her eyes shut, fingers crossed, legs closed,
oblivious to the ladder of her fishnets,

she fingers the red string of her bible,
marks a Psalm before snapping it shut.

Then she's singing again, real loud,
and he's smiling, saying *come as you are*

to the fisher of men
who makes fish clean.

Journey

That's why I'm singing so loud
masking cracks in my voice
papering over missed notes
swallowing down tears
decorating my interior, prettying it up.

Similar to the train ride
when you haven't read the sign
doors slide shut
blocking out orange text:
next train leaves now

– to where exactly?
I'm pretending they bought you
white flowers instead of purple,
and put them in a vase
instead of on the cracked earth.

The City's Eye

I wonder if anyone will notice the splash
when I make contact with the surface.
Water surrounds the eye that blinks itself open,
cars flee over the bridge in a blur of light.

Below, drummers, costumes and bodies writhe, wriggle
and shimmy past; singing, swinging salsa in two time.
Gold, turquoise, magenta, indigo
shoes, hats, belts and buckles flash past.

A child wipes her nose on her collar, a juggler passes
and I trace the lining of my coat repeatedly.
The blue and white lights wink as seductively
as the lapping water of the Thames.

I lean forward until I kiss the surface
and fall into unbroken sleep.

Surname

One Monday you changed your name,
came in and said – *it starts with an M not a V*
erased it from notebooks,
address pads and phone memories.

I'm looking at a picture of you circa 1987,
all dark-eyed and full-lipped.
Stamped across it is *Deptford Office Property* –
but your photo booth look belongs to no one.

Somewhere in your mother's face
sits a mouth that usually pouts on you:
full, fleshy, ripe lips – black lined.
I often wonder what happened to the girl

whose name was discarded
easier than chocolate wrappings
fallen short of the bin,
waiting to be blown away.

She tells me coke was better than it is now,
sprinkled on labia minora,
but only when it is pure –
not cut like they do it these days.

I choke, feigning it is the smoke.
PTA chair, school teacher – mumsy,
fleshy hips jutting to the sides,
fringe flopping over her forehead – stands straight.

The pristine cooker lined with foil,
shiny glinting white and silver.
Her solid pots hiss,
bubble and spit.

All the lines she sniffed,
crystals she heated
til bubbly brown, bottle ready,
drinking in the vapour greedily.

The time she travelled with speed,
tucked in a top knot
shared with strangers
on a Greek beach.

She still has that childish glint of mystery;
takes too long to answer: reminisces
about friends scrabbling on floors
in search of specks of ecstasy.

She adds salt,
her current vice.
Hair swept up in a roll
hurtling towards 50.

Ah Good

10 ah marnin'   yes it was me who spit inna yu cornflakes
                    and swirl it inna di milk.

                    you felt a chill run tru you at 10 fifteen,

                    you choke pan yu cornflakes at 10 thirty.

Ah good.

11 thirty   pavement trip you up - nu so?

1.45pm   coffee spill, cup drop & bruk.

3.45pm   Door slam, window shet, not a breeze…

Ah good.

                    Ah me did sour di milk, choke yu
                    trip yu, mek yu cold
                    mek yu jump

                    ah nuh jumbie, ah nuh duppy – ah me!

                                        and ah good!

Unpicked

Big man sweats,
sweat dripped
landed on my lips
tasted of salt.

Too much salt kills.
Kids should eat less salt than adults.
Adults shouldn't sweat on kids

or have sex with them,

not when they know you
or you call them uncle
especially when they aren't really.
Uncles shouldn't

serve you chips with too much salt.
Too much salt dehydrates you.
Sometimes it kills you years later.

ii. Cherry

Cherry red hymen torn out of you.
You wish it was still there.
So you could give it away
to a boy instead of a man.

Wish you were whole instead of broken,
complete, instead of damaged – good God;
because then, you might be able to fix yourself,
when the cracks start.

But they don't make people glue.
Surgeons can repair hymens now
but haven't figured out how
to make you happy or pretend

you were never broken.

I'll commit a suicide.
Bad grammar stands out
even when spoken quietly.
Particularly through danger.
Suicide: plural or singular?
Got to be singular.
Only happens once, supposedly.

Ironic, all these years later
to find myself thinking.
Thinking of ways
I could do to myself,
what you promised
to do for me.
Still waiting for you, to die.
Liar, liar, liar.

iv. Taste

Breakfast tasted the same as yesterday's,
much like the day before's.
Only today it's flavoured
with the aloes of your memory.

Ten, twenty, forty Dime bars.
Spent my last cent.
Lunch money spent on
chocolate break-times.

Trying to eat a layer of fat around me;
it lands unevenly on breasts and bottom
instead of gut and thighs.
Girl fleshed out into a woman child.

Recently, I've got more cash;
chocolate still tastes good,
breakfast is the same
but I still can't stand the taste of aloes.

v. White tiles

Glaring white tiles, cracked hexagon patterns,
stare down at me.
A tenth of the way home in a motel.
Three-quarters of the way
to crushing my spirit
at the end of half-term.

You fucked me through tears.
Crying:
disappeared me.
Fucked me through tears,
made me invisible.
Fucked a child like a woman
through tears
made me invisible.

Grown woman, still fucked.

vi. Blue

"Birds flying high you know how I feel,
sun in the sky you know how I feel,
breeze drifting on by you know how I feel.
It's a new dawn it's a new day
it's a new life for me
and I'm feeling 'blue'"
- Singing lesson 2006 – Deptford SE8

Mid-lesson – she corrects me:
It's *feeling good.*
I stop, take a deep breath.
Stumble over *feeling good* again.
Been singing it this way for decades,
singing from my belly.
I sing it deep, dirty, low.
I sing it correctly.
Afterwards, mumble under my breath
cos I'm feeling blue.

Not too black
or too fat,

not too old
or too young

not too proud
or too loud.

Super smart
quiet, pretty,

good hair needs
plenty grooming.

Good girls go to heaven
an' bad girls go to hell

keep secrets
never tell.

Noisy tongue will make me dead.

about Warsan Shire

Warsan Shire is a 24 year old Kenyan-born Somali poet, writer, editor and educator who is based in London. Born in 1988, Warsan has read her work extensively all over Britain and internationally – including recent readings in South Africa, Italy, Germany, Canada, America and Kenya. Her poems have been published in Wasafiri, Magma and Poetry Review and in the anthology 'The Salt Book of Younger Poets' (Salt, 2011). She is the current poetry editor at SPOOK magazine and, in 2012, she represented Somalia at the Poetry Parnassus, the festival of the world poets at the Southbank, London. Warsan's poetry has been translated into Italian, Spanish and Portuguese. She is a Complete Works II poet. and winner of the inaugural 2013 Brunel University African Poetry Prize.

author statement

Working with my editor Jacob Sam- La Rose on the manuscript for 'Teaching My Mother How To Give Birth' was an education on care and detail. I'm so grateful to have been in the hands of such a dedicated and supportive person, who is also a brilliant poet. He taught to look at my work as if it were not my own. Also, to view it as a body of work, and not just random poems compiled together. I began writing the manuscript as a teenager and with his help, watched it grow in to something I am proud to call my own. It was an honour to have one of my favourite poets be both my mentor and editor. flipped eye is a family and I'm glad to be home.

kudos
winner of
Brunel University African Poetry Prize (2013)
selected as
Poetry Parnassus Poet, Somalia (2012)

Teaching My Mother How To Give Birth

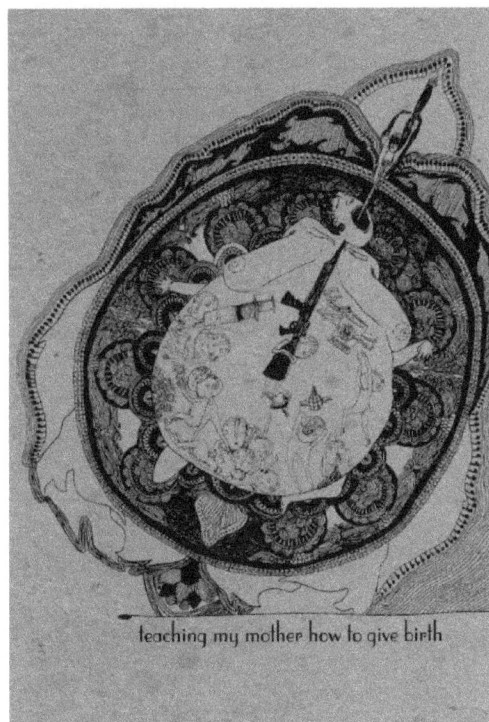

teaching my mother how to give birth

Warsan Shire

First Published: 2011
Series Number: 10
Editor: Jacob Sam-La Rose

Mother, loosen my tongue or adorn me with a lighter burden.
— Audre Lorde

Teaching My Mother How to Give Birth

I have my mother's mouth and my father's eyes; on my face they are still together.

What Your Mother Told You After Your Father Left

I did not beg him to stay
because I was begging God
that he would not leave.

Your Mother's First Kiss

The first boy to kiss your mother later raped women
when the war broke out. She remembers hearing this
from your uncle, then going to your bedroom and lying
down on the floor. You were at school.

Your mother was sixteen when he first kissed her.
She held her breath for so long that she blacked out.
On waking she found her dress was wet and sticking
to her stomach, half moons bitten into her thighs.

That same evening she visited a friend, a girl
who fermented wine illegally in her bedroom.
When your mother confessed *I've never been touched
like that before*, the friend laughed, mouth bloody with grapes,
then plunged a hand between your mother's legs.

Last week, she saw him driving the number 18 bus,
his cheek a swollen drumlin, a vine scar dragging itself
across his mouth. You were with her, holding a bag
of dates to your chest, heard her let out a deep moan
when she saw how much you looked like him.

Things We Had Lost in the Summer

The summer my cousins return from Nairobi,
we sit in a circle by the oak tree in my aunt's garden.
They look older. Amel's hardened nipples push through
the paisley of her blouse, minarets calling men to worship.
When they left, I was twelve years old and swollen
with the heat of waiting. We hugged at the departure gate,
waifs with bird chests clinking like wood, boyish,
long skirted figurines waiting to grow
into our hunger.

My mother uses her quiet voice on the phone:
Are they all okay? Are they healing well?
She doesn't want my father to overhear.

Juwariyah, my age, leans in and whispers
I've started my period. Her hair is in my mouth when
I try to move in closer– *how does it feel?*
She turns to her sisters and a laugh that is not hers
stretches from her body like a moan.
She is more beautiful than I can remember.
One of them pushes my open knees closed.
Sit like a girl. I finger the hole in my shorts,
shame warming my skin.

In the car, my mother stares at me through the
rear view mirror, the leather sticks to the back of my
thighs. I open my legs like a well-oiled door,
daring her to look at me and give me
what I had not lost: a name.

Maymuun's Mouth

Maymuun lost her accent with the help of her local Community College. Most evenings she calls me long distance to discuss the pros and cons of heating molasses in the microwave to remove body hair. Her new voice is sophisticated. She has taken to dancing in front of strangers. She lives next door to a Dominican who speaks to her in Spanish whenever they pass each other in hallways. I know she smiles at him, front teeth stained from the fluoride in the water back home. She's experiencing new things. We understand. We've received the photos of her standing by a bridge, the baby hair she'd hated all her life slicked down like ravines. Last week her answering machine picked up. I imagined her hoisted by the waist, wearing stockings, learning to kiss with her new tongue.

Grandfather's Hands

Your grandfather's hands were brown.
Your grandmother kissed each knuckle,

circled an island into his palm
and told him which parts they would share,
which part they would leave alone.

She wet a finger to draw where the ocean would be
on his wrist, kissed him there,
named the ocean after herself.

Your grandfather's hands were slow but urgent.
Your grandmother dreamt them,

a clockwork of fingers finding places to own–
under the tongue, collarbone, bottom lip,
arch of foot.

Your grandmother names his fingers after seasons–
index finger, a wave of heat,
middle finger, rainfall.

Some nights his thumb is the moon
nestled just under her rib.

Your grandparents often found themselves
in dark rooms, mapping out
each other's bodies,

claiming whole countries
with their mouths.

Bone

I find a girl the height of a small wail
living in our spare room. She looks the way I did when I was fifteen
full of pulp and pepper.
She spends all day up in the room
measuring her thighs.

Her body is one long sigh.
You notice her in the hallway.
Later that night while we lay beside one another
listening to her throw up in our bathroom,
you tell me you want to save her.
Of course you do;
This is what she does best:
makes you sick with the need
to help.

We have the same lips,
she and I,
the kind men think about
when they are with their wives.
She is starving.
You look straight at me when she tells us
how her father likes to punch girls
in the face.

I can hear you in our spare room with her.
What is she hungry for?
What can you fill her up with?
What can you do, that you would not do for me?
I count my ribs before I go to sleep.

Snow

My father was a drunk. He married my mother
the month he came back from Russia
with whiskey in his blood.
On their wedding night, he whispered
into her ear about jet planes and snow.
He said the word in Russian;
my mother blinked back tears and spread her palms
across his shoulder blades like the wings
of a plane. Later, breathless, he laid his head
on her thigh and touched her,
brought back two fingers glistening,
showed her from her own body
what the colour of snow was closest to.

Birds

Sofia used pigeon blood on her wedding night.
Next day, over the phone, she told me
how her husband smiled when he saw the sheets,

that he gathered them under his nose,
closed his eyes and dragged his tongue over the stain.
She mimicked his baritone, how he whispered

her name– Sofia,
pure, chaste, untouched.
We giggled over the static.

After he had praised her, she smiled, rubbed his head,
imagined his mother back home, parading
these siren sheets through the town,

waving at balconies, torso swollen with pride,
her arms fleshy wings bound to her body,
ignorant of flight.

Beauty

My older sister soaps between her legs, her hair
a prayer of curls. When she was my age, she stole
the neighbour's husband, burnt his name into her skin.
For weeks she smelt of cheap perfume and dying flesh.

It's 4 a.m. and she winks at me, bending over the sink,
her small breasts bruised from sucking.
She smiles, pops her gum before saying
boys are haram, don't ever forget that.

Some nights I hear her in her room screaming.
We play Surah Al-Baqarah to drown her out.
Anything that leaves her mouth sounds like sex.
Our mother has banned her from saying God's name.

The Kitchen

Half a papaya and a palmful of sesame oil;
  lately, your husband's mind has been elsewhere.

Honeyed dates, goat's milk;
  you want to quiet the bloating of salt.

Coconut and ghee butter;
  he kisses the back of your neck at the stove.

Cayenne and roasted pine nuts;
  you offer him the hollow of your throat.

Saffron and rosemary;
  you don't ask him her name.

Vine leaves and olives;
  you let him lift you by the waist.

Cinnamon and tamarind;
  lay you down on the kitchen counter.

Almonds soaked in rose water;
  your husband is hungry.

Sweet mangoes and sugared lemon;
  he had forgotten the way you taste.

Sour dough and cumin;
  but she cannot make him eat, like you.

Fire

i

The morning you were made to leave
she sat on the front steps,
dress tucked between her thighs,
a packet of Marlboro Lights
near her bare feet, painting her nails
until the polish curdled.
Her mother phoned–

What do you mean he hit you?
Your father hit me all the time
but I never left him.
He pays the bills
and he comes home at night,
what more do you want?

Later that night she picked the polish off
with her front teeth until the bed you shared
for seven years seemed speckled with glitter
and blood.

ii

On the drive to the hotel, you remember
the funeral you went to as a little boy,
double burial for a couple who
burned to death in their bedroom.
The wife had been visited
by her husband's lover,
a young and beautiful woman who paraded
her naked body in the couple's kitchen,
lifting her dress to expose breasts
mottled with small fleshy marks,
a back sucked and bruised, then dressed herself
and walked out of the front door.
The wife, waiting for her husband to come home,
doused herself in lighter fluid. On his arrival
she jumped on him, wrapping her legs around
his torso. The husband, surprised at her sudden urge,
carried his wife to the bedroom, where
she straddled him on their bed, held his face
against her chest and lit a match.

iii

A young man greets you in the elevator.
He smiles like he has pennies hidden in his cheeks.
You're looking at his shoes when he says
the rooms in this hotel are sweltering.
Last night in bed I swear I thought
my body was on fire.

When We Last Saw Your Father

H
e was sitting in the hospital parking lot
in a borrowed car, counting the windows
of the building, guessing which one
was glowing with his mistake.

You Were Conceived

On the night of our secret wedding
when he held me in his mouth like a promise
until his tongue grew tired and fell asleep,
I lay awake to keep the memory alive.

In the morning I begged him back to bed.
Running late, he kissed my ankles and left.
I stayed like a secret in his bed for days
until his mother found me.

I showed her my gold ring,
I stood in front of her naked,
waved my hands in her face.
She sank to the floor and cried.

At his funeral, no one knew my name.
I sat behind his aunts,
they sucked on dates soaked in oil.
The last thing he tasted was me.

Trying to Swim With God

Istaqfurulah

My mother says this city is slowly killing all our women;
practising back strokes at the local swimming pool.
I think of Kadija, how her body had failed her
on the way down from the block of flats.

The instructor tells us that the longest
a human being has held their breath under water
is 19 minutes and 21 seconds. At home in the bath,
my hair swells to the surface like vines, I stay submerged
until I can no longer stand it, think of all the things
I have allowed to slip through my fingers.

Inna lillahi Wa inna ilaihi Rajioon.

My mother says no one can fight it –
the body returning to God,

but the way she fell, face first,
in the dirt,
mouth full of earth,
 air, teeth, blood,
wearing a white cotton baati,
hair untied and smoked with ounsi,
I wonder if Kadija believed

she was going to float.

Questions for Miriam

Were you ever lonely?

Did you tell people that songs weren't
the same as a warm body, a soft mouth?
Did you know how to say no to young men
who cried outside your hotel rooms?
Did you listen to the songs they wrote,
tongues wet with praise for you?

What sweaty bars did you begin in?
Did you see them holding bottles by the neck,
hair on their arms rising as your notes hovered
above their heads?
Did you know of the girls who sang into their fists
mimicking your brilliance?

Did they know that you were only human?

My parents played your music at their wedding.
Called you Makeba, never Miriam, never first name,
always singer. Never wife, daughter, mother,
never lover, aching.

Did you tell people that songs weren't the same
as a warm body or a soft mouth? Miriam,
I've heard people using your songs as prayer,
begging god in falsetto. You were a city

exiled from skin, your mouth a burning church.

Conversations About Home

(at the Deportation Centre)

Well, I think home spat me out, the blackouts and curfews like tongue against loose tooth. God, do you know how difficult it is, to talk about the day your own city dragged you by the hair, past the old prison, past the school gates, past the burning torsos erected on poles like flags? When I meet others like me I recognise the longing, the missing, the memory of ash on their faces. No one leaves home unless home is the mouth of a shark. I've been carrying the old anthem in my mouth for so long that there's no space for another song, another tongue or another language. I know a shame that shrouds, totally engulfs. I tore up and ate my own passport in an airport hotel. I'm bloated with language I can't afford to forget.

*

They ask me *how did you get here?* Can't you see it on my body? The Libyan desert red with immigrant bodies, the Gulf of Aden bloated, the city of Rome with no jacket. I hope the journey meant more than miles because all of my children are in the water. I thought the sea was safer than the land. I want to make love, but my hair smells of war and running and running. I want to lay down, but these countries are like uncles who touch you when you're young and asleep. Look at all these borders, foaming at the mouth with bodies broken and desperate. I'm the colour of hot sun on the face, my mother's remains were never buried. I spent days and nights in the stomach of the truck; I did not come out the same. Sometimes it feels like someone else is wearing my body.

*

I know a few things to be true. I do not know where I am going, where I have come from is disappearing, I am unwelcome and my beauty is not beauty here. My body is burning with the shame of not belonging, my body is longing. I am the sin of memory and the absence of memory. I watch the news and my mouth becomes a sink full of blood. The lines, the forms, the people at the desks, the calling cards, the immigration officer, the looks on the street, the cold settling deep into my bones, the English classes at night, the distance I am from home. But Alhamdulilah all of this is better than the scent of a woman completely on fire, or a truckload of men who look like my father, pulling out my teeth and nails, or fourteen men between my legs, or a gun, or a promise, or a lie, or his name, or his manhood in my mouth.

*

I hear them say *go home*, I hear them say *fucking immigrants, fucking refugees*. Are they really this arrogant? Do they not know that stability is like a lover with a sweet mouth upon your body one second; the next you are a tremor lying on the floor covered in rubble and old currency waiting for its return. All I can say is, I was once like you, the apathy, the pity, the ungrateful placement and now my home is the mouth of a shark, now my home is the barrel of a gun. I'll see you on the other side.

Old Spice

Every Sunday afternoon he dresses in his old army uniform,
tells you the name of every man he killed.
His knuckles are unmarked graves.

Visit him on a Tuesday and he will describe
the body of every woman he could not save.
He'll say she looked like your mother
and you will feel a storm in your stomach.

Your grandfather is from another generation–
Russian degrees and a school yard Cuban national anthem,
communism and religion. Only music makes him cry now.

He married his first love, her with the long curls down
to the small of her back. Sometimes he would
pull her to him, those curls wrapped around his hand
like rope.

He lives alone now. Frail, a living memory
reclining in a seat, the room orbiting around him.
You visit him but never have anything to say.
When he was your age he was a man.
You retreat into yourself whenever he says your name.

Your mother's father,
the almost martyr,
can load a gun under water
in under four seconds.

Even his wedding night was a battlefield.
A Swiss knife, his young bride,
his sobs as he held Italian linen between her legs.

His face is a photograph left out in the sun,
the henna of his beard, the silver of his eyebrows
the wilted handkerchief, the kufi and the cane.

Your grandfather is dying.
He begs you *Take me home yaqay,
I just want to see it one last time;*
you don't know how to tell him that it won't be
anything like the way he left it.

My Foreign Wife is Dying and Does Not Want To Be Touched

My wife is a ship docking from war.
The doctor maps out her body in ink,
holding up her breast with two fingers, explains
what needs to be removed, that maybe we can keep
the nipple. Her body is a flooding home.
We are afraid. We want to know
what the water will take away from us,
what the earth will claim as its own.
I lick my lips and she looks at the floor.

Later, at home, she calls her sister.
They talk about curses, the evil eye, their aunt
who drowned, all the money they need
to send back. It is morning when she comes to bed
and lets me touch her. I am like a thirsty child
against her chest, her skin
is parchment, dry and cracking.

My wife sits on the hospital bed.
Gown and body together: 41 kilos.
She is a boat docking in from war,
her body, a burning village, a prison
with open gates. She won't let me hold her
now, when she needs it most.

We stare at the small television in the corner of the room.
I think of all the images she must carry in her body,
how the memory hardens into a tumour.
Apathy is the same as war,
it all kills you, she says.
Slow like cancer in the breast
or fast like a machete in the neck.

Ugly

Your daughter is ugly.
She knows loss intimately,
carries whole cities in her belly.

As a child, relatives wouldn't hold her.
She was splintered wood and sea water.
She reminded them of the war.

On her fifteenth birthday you taught her
how to tie her hair like rope
and smoke it over burning frankincense.

You made her gargle rosewater
and while she coughed, said
macaanto girls like you shouldn't smell
of lonely or empty.

You are her mother.
Why did you not warn her,
hold her like a rotting boat
and tell her that men will not love her
if she is covered in continents,
if her teeth are small colonies,
if her stomach is an island
if her thighs are borders?

What man wants to lie down
and watch the world burn
in his bedroom?

Your daughter's face is a small riot,
her hands are a civil war,

a refugee camp behind each ear,
a body littered with ugly things.

But God,
doesn't she wear
the world well?

Tea With Our Grandmothers

The morning your habooba died
I thought of my ayeeyo, the woman
I was named after, Warsan Baraka,
skin dark like tamarind flesh,
who died grinding cardamom
waiting for her sons to come home and
raise the loneliness they'd left behind;

or my mother's mother, Noura
with the honeyed laugh, who
broke cinnamon barks between
her palms, nursing her husband's
stroke, her sister's cancer and
her own bad back with broken
Swahili and stubborn Italian;

and Doris, the mother of your
English rose, named after
the daughter of Oceanus and Tethys
the Welsh in your blood, from the land
of Cymry, your grandmother who
dreams of clotted cream in her tea
through the swell of diabetes;

then your habooba Al-Sura,
God keep her, with three lines on
each cheek, a tally of surviving,
the woman who cooled your tea
pouring it like the weight of deeds
between bowl and cup, until the steam
would rise like a ghost.

To my daughter I will say,
'when the men come, set yourself on fire'.

Notes

Surah Al Baqarah — A chapter in the Qu'ran, used to ward off evil.

Habooba — Arabic word meaning beloved woman, used as the word for grandmother in Sudan.

Ayeeyo — Somali word for Grandmother.

Macaanto — Somali term of endearment, meaning sweetness.

Inna lillahi Wa inna ilaihi Rajioon — Arabic; To Allah we belong and truly, to Him we shall return.

Baati — Long cotton Somali nightdress.

Ounsi — The somali tradition to burn frankincense and myrrh over hot coal, releasing aroma through smoke.

Istaqfurulah — Arabic, Allah forgive my sins.

Yaqay — Somali word used to emphasise emotion/urgency in speech.

Haram — Legally forbidden by Islamic law.

Kufi — A brimless short rounded cap worn mainly by African men.

Baraka — Blessings

Alhamdulilah — Praise be to Allah.

acknowledgements

Inua Ellams dedicates his work *to capsules of walking water – sculpted by the wind.*

Jessica Horn dedicates her work to *my mother and her kinswomen who embody a graceful fire. To Nii Ayikwei Parkes, writer/publisher/acivist extraordinaire, for having faith in my words. To Kevin Quashie and the women in our poetry collective at Smith College for nourishing the journey. To Ina, Oul and David for inspiring poems in this collection.   To my grandfather Timothy Bazarrabusa, writer, teacher, diplomat, government minister, mountaineer and parliamentarian, whom I never met but hope to learn from.   To women everywhere, because the world belongs to us as well.*

Nick Makoha thanks *Johanna and our children for their love at all times, and Roger Robinson, Malika Booker and Jacob Sam-La Rose for relating to me as a writer and not settling for less.*

Nii Ayikwei Parkes would like to thank *Marrianne San Miguel for bearing with me during obsessive editing marathons, Jacob Sam-La Rose and Niall O'Sullivan for agreeing to share my workload and Cara Lai, for a wonderful job of proofreading this anthology during her internship with flipped eye.*

Denise Saul says this book is *for Eris*

Truth Thomas wrote this book *for God, Mom, Cherry, Soweto, Randall, Ethelbert, Medina, Shaggy, Nii and Doors of Return, Bruce, Martin Luther King, Jr. Community Church, the Funky Cold Workshop family, the UK family, Derrick, Fred, Alan & the world.*

and

The flipped eye crew thanks *you for reading*

www.ingramcontent.com/pod-product-compliance
Lightning Source LLC
Chambersburg PA
CBHW030728150426
42813CB00051B/343